DAY TRADING OPTIONS

for A Living

-:-:-:-

The Complete Guide to Day Trading Tools, Techniques, Strategies, Money and Risk Management

- WILLIAM RICHARDS –

COPYRIGHT WILLIAM RICHARDS © 2020

ALL RIGHTS RESERVED

No part of this publication may be reproduced, distributed, or transmitted in any form or by any means, including photocopying, recording, or other electronic or mechanical methods, or by any information storage and retrieval system without the prior written permission of the publisher, except in the case of very brief quotations embodied in critical reviews and certain other non-commercial uses permitted by copyright law.

TABLE OF CONTENTS

INTRODUCTION   5

HISTORY OF OPTIONS TRADING   5

THINGS NEEDED TO BEGIN DAY TRADING   12

MINDSET OF A SUCCESSFUL DAY TRADER   23

EXAMPLE OF PSYCHOLOGY TRADING - INTUITION   50

DIFFERENCES BETWEEN LONG AND SHORT-DAY TRADING   54

DIFFERENCE BETWEEN TRADING AND INVESTING   58

LIVE TRADING IS POSSIBLE? 10 TIPS TO DO IT   62

10 TIPS FOR TRADING A LIVING   66

WHAT ARE OPTIONS   77

WHAT ARE BINARY OPTIONS: EXAMPLE, ADVANTAGES AND RISKS   77
EXAMPLE OF INVESTMENT IN BINARY OPTIONS   85
EXAMPLE OF TRADING WITH BINARY OPTIONS   91

BUYING AND SELLING OPTIONS: STRATEGIES AND ANALYSIS   94

BEST ONLINE TRADING STRATEGIES	**104**
THE ANALYSIS OF SUPPORTS AND RESISTANCES	117
TREND ANALYSIS	119
THE DOUBLE ZERO STRATEGY	121
THE BREAK-OUT TECHNIQUE	123
THOMAS JEGU AND THE "U" STRATEGY	124
LET'S START: TRADING ONLINE	**127**
TECHNICAL ANALYSIS	128
FUNDAMENTAL ANALYSIS	149
TRADING SIGNALS (RELIABLE)	171
EXAMPLE OF SIGNALS WITH THE MOVING AVERAGE	181
FAMOUS TRADERS, NAMES, STORIES AND STRATEGIES	**186**

INTRODUCTION

History of Options Trading

When we talk about online trading we are talking about a very dynamic and future-oriented world. Both on the future of quotations and on the future as regards general economic trends. But rarely does one turn to the past except to apply strategies on historical charts.

The past, however, sometimes brings with its valuable information and teachings that should not be underestimated. In this book we do not pretend to provide the lessons of the past as regards online trading but only to tell how it all started.

It all began in 1993, when, thanks also to the initial spread of the internet on the American stock exchange, it was decided to put quotes online and the possibility of interacting no longer only through a real-life financial broker but also through an online broker.

From 2000 begins the important growth in the number of operators who approach trading from home and 2000 sees the first bubble of internet stocks comparable only to the speculative bubble of tulip bulbs in the Netherlands of 1600 which came to cost as a property.

The online market, at that time, was not particularly thriving from the point of view of online trading platforms and internet connections were a huge drag (very few had a fast line). Then over time the number of people interested in online trading grew and consequently the online brokers grew with increasingly performing platforms that allowed more and more functions.

This growth took place until the 2007 bubble burst (subprime bubble) where many traders got hurt. Since 2007, with various economic and financial crises that have "plagued" the world, even the number of traders has not grown as before. Before 2007, there was someone who speculated that over time each person would manage their savings online. Obviously, this prediction has so far proved false.

Surely, with the end of this economic crisis and with the advent of new growth (we hope for a new economic boom) the number of people who will approach online trading will again increase.

Online trading etymology

More and more often we hear about online trading as a new investment method, but what is it? Let's start from the etymology: trading means to trade, therefore trading online literally means trading online, or on the internet.

Obviously, the word "trade" is quite generic, so we can narrow it down to define what kind of trade is understood in common usage.

Online trading involves the purchase and sale of financial instruments such as stocks, futures, government bonds, bonds and more.

This new investment system has become something of a synonym for how to make money online, considering that all it takes to implement it is a simple Internet connection and a PC with very basic system requirements. To make money on the internet there are few really effective ways (besides work, of course), and online trading is one of them.

Among the main advantages of this practice we can include the low commission costs for the investor, who can therefore count on a much higher net profit than the old trades. Another important advantage is the constant availability of market data, updated every second by specialized sites and software platforms for trading.

If the financial market and investments are your passion, you can't miss the opportunity to try online trading at least once. This practice is now on the agenda and more and more enthusiasts are making it a real job, before and after retirement.

We hear a lot about online trading and that it is a way to make money by investing in the stock market.

Online trading is actually a way of investing capital from the comfort of your home or through a portable device with the markets and the stock exchange.

The trader therefore buys and sells financial products, which also have low commissions and allow you to keep market and investment trends under control in real time. The British have abbreviated it by calling it with the acronym "TOL" which stands for "to trade" that is to trade.

You cannot improvise trader and to do online trading you need not only a thorough knowledge of investments, markets and quotes, but you must constantly study the charts and have financial intuition. The choices you make when you decide to invest capital are determined n you for successful operations.

Online trading can be done while the markets open. But you can also do the "extraordinary".

Online trading therefore consists in negotiating various financial products on as many markets, knowing the tools to invest and those available to the investor (especially the share of capital).

To trade online it is necessary to open an account with a broker, which must be checked regarding the regulation.

Today, with home banking and the tools offered by the internet, it is easy to do everything on the web, directly from a desk.

The trader's job is to keep under control, through his platform, everything that can positively or negatively affect a stock or an entire financial sector, focusing on all relevant news concerning the micro and macro economy and which act on market trends.

Before any investment you need to have reliable information on associated companies, starting with the opinions of economic analysts to continue with capital increases, rating by agencies and a series of variables to monitor. Skills are obviously acquired over the years and therefore with experience.

Online trading is a way to deal with the purchase or sale of bonds, government bonds, features, etc. and the choice of the modus operandi is fundamental, which can lead to success by paying close attention to the times and changes or corrections to be made to each investment, sometimes in real time, if market trends are uncertain and affected by strong fluctuations. One might think that the birth of online trading is closely linked to that of the internet and the implementation of web banking systems.

This is not exactly the case as the roots of online trading go back to 1993. The need arose to speed up the accounting systems for which the so-called "executed" had to be transcribed. The regulation of this new way of making investments and moving capital had the effect of increasing those who tried their hand at online trading, also thanks to the spread of the internet and the increasingly efficient connection speed.

The evolution of online trading

Over the years online trading has evolved allowing access to new financial instruments not only to professional traders, but also to simple investors who, through a platform (usually the one offered by their bank through home banking), want to invest capital.

Contrary to what one might think, online trading are not investments made just one day to speculate, but they have various ways in which to use capital even with maturities of 10 years. The calculation of the risk is of course in relation to the investment you want to make, to how much you are willing to lose but above all to earn.

Online trading today offers different ways to invest and, for those new to the sector, there are terminologies that you need to get to know because there is a real "jargon". Each trader can choose the type of approach that according to his judgment suits the investment. As mentioned, you can choose to make financial transactions that last only one day, opening and closing in the time between the opening and closing of the markets.

This type of operation is that of "day trading" and is chosen when you are not willing to do the so-called "overnight", that is to leave the operation open overnight and expose it in the morning to any news that could negatively affect the markets and the quotes. It is very similar to open trading, that is the investments that are made by entering the platform only following an important news or an economic- financial data that could yield a profit. It is also possible to aim for immediate profit with trades lasting a few seconds and which are called "scalpers".

Then there are the long-term investors who instead focus on a stock with few fluctuations and who think that it can be profitable over time. In this case we speak of investment even at 10 years.

For all these methods there are real strategies to be acquired over time and which allow you to enter the world of finance and capital movements, also learning to manage risk.

THINGS NEEDED TO BEGIN DAY TRADING

Since trading has landed on the net, the activity has been carried out not only by experienced investors, but also by ordinary people who, through the internet, are able to learn both theoretical and practical knowledge to invest.

Online trading, also known by the abbreviation TOL, is a new financial system that uses the internet to carry out various types of transactions, such as the purchase and sale of movable and immovable property.

Directly from home or from your office you can interact with the world of the stock market and invest your money. An inexpensive way to increase your earnings, but it's always good to keep your eyes peeled. This is the first piece of advice that should be given to newbies!

The commissions are lower and also you have the possibility to access charts in real time as well as you can consult the technical analysis and quotes. However, we must always understand the dynamics of the markets to avoid large losses.

How does online trading work?

Most investors devote hours to TOL so that you can invest in equities with complete peace of mind and conscience.

Since the internet is the main tool to carry out these operations, the commission cost is certainly very low for those who invest. Furthermore, there are many means offered to those who dedicate themselves to the T OL to monitor the securities and get information on the stock market trend. For each share it is also possible to receive corporate news, such as: new contracts, capital increases, reduction or increase in target price, ratings and opinions from analysts. Without excluding the fact that there are sections dedicated purely to budgets, finance, mathematics and statistics.

Before going into and using the TOL, you also need to know the tools we have available to proceed with the investment. It is possible to rely on some companies to avoid possible traps, scams and financial speculation.

Where can you invest?

It is possible to invest both in Europe and in America but we must always refer to the services we have activated on our online platform.

What should I connect to?

Those who are not professional investors can take advantage of home banking or online platforms where it will be possible to make investments, make payments and bank transfers, view the account statement. When we talk about home banking, we mean the first step to start with online trading.

A second alternative is to enter into a contract at the branch of the bank for which you intend to operate. Once the forms have been downloaded directly online, the contract is filled in and signed, which must then be returned to the credit institution. Once the contract has been registered, the bank will provide a username and password. Once the access data has been obtained, it will be possible to start the online trading activity.

How many ways to operate are there for online trading?

Scalping is the entry and exit of the market, usually with stocks and several times throughout the day. The scalper is therefore the one who uses the book constantly. Here the money indicates how much we are willing to pay to buy the stock; the letter is the seller's request for money and therefore equals the selling price of the security. On the left side of the book the amount of money, the number of shares and the purchase price are marked.

By Day Trading we mean the purchase of a share on a given day after following that product for a certain period. In this circumstance, the proponent of the operation is strongly convinced of the title and its value. Therefore, he has no doubts about his investment which he considers profitable.

Open traders are those who enter the market in a completely random way, perhaps after reading some data or news around. As for, however, long investors are those who believe in a particular stock and claim that it can rise over a medium-long time frame.

Trading is for some traders a real job, a full-fledged activity. Tactics and strategies are developed in order to be more and more precise and skilled on the front of the bag. For those who are just starting out, there are numerous online courses that help you understand the main financial movements until you interact with an experienced trader.

Live Trading is one of the main courses that allows you to practice and carry out transactions with real money. Just connect to specific sites, sign up to attend a lesson or live trading course. The online version allows, in fact, to take part in the courses from the comfort of home, even if it is possible to participate in individual or group lessons, ideal for both novice and professional traders.

What are the most common mistakes when it comes to trading?

Since trading has landed on the network, the activity is carried out not only by experienced investors, but also by ordinary people who, through the internet, are able to learn both theoretical and practical knowledge to invest.

In the first moments of activity it is normal to make mistakes. One of the most common is to confuse online trading with gambling, a bet; the fact that there is money at stake almost creates confusion between gaming and investing. But unlike the stroke of luck, valid for gambling, the market has a logic to follow and understand.

Furthermore, during operations it happens to lose control and lucidity. You have to be careful and try to always be rational in order to proceed keeping in mind the costs, benefits and risks.

The advice of the experts is not to improvise, but to plan every single step. The trader should first know the amount of money he is willing to lose; the decision comes suddenly and we must not give way to emotionality and above all to the fear of losing. Of great importance to start the business is certainly the training with its updating. We must first study and then operate on the market. According to experts it is necessary to study a strategy and always keep up with new techniques.

Trading has grown in recent years also thanks to the current economic situation and the high unemployment rate that now grips our country. To embark on this new "virtual" financial activity are mainly young people, but not always know the rules, and logic governing stock markets. One of the first steps is in fact to practice, and therefore to start a simulation to train before obtaining results. We are talking about simulated trading which represents a real training during which the trader is able to simulate investments and market operations, making use of a special platform.

This phase of the simulation is fundamental for the learning of those who are preparing to become a trader; obviously in this obligatory stage the use of money is not foreseen. According to some, the simulation is however different from reality as there are no anxiety, doubts and fears on the pitch that will instead be present when you really take the field and operate on the market.

The simulated trader allows the user to get in touch with the platform, to analyse investments in a more rational way, to buy the product that increases in value and to sell it when it goes down. However, there are no prizes and punishments that could bring the person into the perspective of stock market speculation.

Another variant of trading: trading with binary options

Trading with binary options is the system used to make money faster. It is essentially based on hourly or daily contracts and it is invested not on the difference between buying and selling, typical of classic trading, but on the prediction that it is verifiable or not. The danger of binary options trading lies above all in its main feature, which is its unpredictability. Since the transaction takes place in a very short time, it is not possible to predict in detail the performance of the contract on which you are investing. This type of investment almost takes the form of a roulette wheel. If we have savings of 10,000 euros available, the smartest move is never to invest, more than a thousand euros. It is very important to rely on a platform that is simple to use and above all safe. The second option is to invest different amounts on the same contract or make small diversified investments on various contracts.

Trading and platforms

Each trader can rely on a type of platform on which to invest their money. The main solutions are: the Mot, the trading platforms offered by brokers and those of banks.

The trading platforms offered by brokers can be born either as the result of a convention or because they are owned by them. One of the recognized and most efficient software is definitely MetaTrader. There are both marker maker brokers where coverage for orders is always offered and brokers who only act as intermediaries and are therefore more difficult to use.

Finally, many banks provide software for trading. They are slightly more expensive as platforms than those of traditional brokers, but have greater protection and assistance.

Trading and scams: how to avoid them?

In recent years, the phenomenon of online trading has been enjoying great success all over the world. If on the one hand there are those who have always been fascinated by the world of the stock exchange and the financial markets, on the other hand there are those who hope to be able to improve their financial situation. The confirmation of this new financial method is undoubtedly also linked to the recent economic crisis. If until the 90s we were used to imagining stock market operators screaming to buy or sell shares, now it is possible to carry out the same activity with an internet connection and a PC. It is obviously advisable to realize how relevant both experience and the study of basic notions are.

The internet can be a real "trap" with announcements and messages that proclaim earnings in a simple and immediate way.

It has happened that inexperienced traders have stumbled upon these traps by brokers who have offices in tax havens and who delude people in their first steps. History teaches that there are many traders who, driven by the illusion and persuasive force of fake brokers, have decided to invest all their savings in trading accounts which will then reveal ghosts.

The ending of the stories is the same for everyone: you find yourself without a single penny on the bill.

What must be done to avoid being scammed?

The brokers, promoters of these scams, seek as a victim a trader who is inexperienced and who must completely trust him to proceed with the various financial operations. To be sure that the broker with which we intend to open an account is in possession of the appropriate licenses to offer financial services, we must try to carry out various searches, also referring to forums, blogs and comments left by other traders who have opened an online trading counter at the same broker.

Our final goal will be to be sure of its total reliability and transparency.

Social Trading

Social trading is a new way to access the financial markets, essentially allowing traders to benefit from the skills of others by offering you the opportunity to follow other traders around the world, find their strategies and see how they operate.

It is a bit like Facebook where everyone spies on friends or acquaintances, obviously it is very advantageous as it allows us to spy on the best brokers. eToro, to date, for example, is the largest online trading community in the world, and offers its social trading platform.

Social trading is undoubtedly the first step towards the future of the world of financial investments.

What is social trading?

The social trading network allows the trader to use a social network according to their needs and the idea of how to invest. An important tool capable of making people observe, follow and copy. As with any social network, the main action is to observe.

This phase allows you to view the trading actions of other brokers at any time. Information is one of the main elements of trading actions.

It is necessary to always keep up to date on the actions of other traders to receive suggestions on which strategies to follow or which actions to buy. Following traders allows you to monitor them: any news will appear on the bulletin board. Following brokers is part of a professional tactic that will allow you to increase your skills.

Some platforms also highlight the most followed brokers in order to find the best traders. To get more benefits from social trading, one of the most important steps is certainly to copy the activity of other traders in order to make the strategy their own. This action allows you to think more adequately about what are the best strategies to adopt.

MINDSET OF A SUCCESSFUL DAY TRADER

How to manage emotions

Some say that all diseases have a common origin: the mind. This statement is absolutely true in the case of trading. The trader can know all the trend indicators, all the tactics and signals, make the predictions correctly, but he enters the market and all this knowledge ceases to be important - he simply lets his emotions take over.

The science that studies the behaviour of traders and tries to offer them the keys to good emotion management is called Trading Psychology.

Trading Psychology - Common mistakes and misconceptions

The world of financial investments is often compared to a casino: emotions, passions, bets ... When a trader begins his career is really easy to get into the vortex of their own passions and emotions, only a trained professional can manage these components, often typical of this practice. Keep in mind that every trader feels emotions when he loses or when he wins, but the pros stand out for their Spartan endurance and control of their feelings and emotional reactions.

There is an unwritten law valid for all those who wish to trade:

> The higher the level of emotionality, the lower the work efficiency

It seems like a simple thing: controlling your feelings. However, the mechanisms for suppressing all of our emotions and experiences are very complicated to apply. In the initial phase, it can be nearly impossible to refrain from the joy of winning or the worry of failure, but if you learn how to reduce your emotionality it will be much easier to achieve success as a trader. This is the psychology of trading. Otherwise you run the risk of adding to the sad statistics of those who have abandoned halfway.

It is important to remember that unlike in a casino, where everything depends on luck, in trading you have to keep a cool head at all times as we have to decide the course of trading, stop it completely or double the investment. If these decisions are made quickly and without thinking, then it will become a game of luck, nothing else.

Our job is to make a profit, not to win a prize. Being lucky at any given moment is undoubtedly a pleasant prospect, but too ephemeral and too illusory. This is why it is important to answer several questions before starting to trade: How do we feel about trading? If we want to earn money constantly then we will have to abandon the idea of PLAYING on the market.

Of course, we shouldn't expect all traders to become newsboys, waving their arms in the markets as we often see in movies and even on the news. But it is a good image for us to have an idea of how the emotions within us behave. The main difficulty in defeating the enemy is identifying him.

Trading Psychology - The main emotions of the trader

The trader's main enemies are his own emotions. Traditionally there are four emotional manifestations related to trading, they are:

- ✓ Fear
- ✓ Greed
- ✓ The hope
- ✓ The euphoria

Strangely and unlike other contexts in life, positive emotions do not help the trader and lead to "stupid things", taking actions that he had not even remotely planned to do.

Trading Psychology - Fear

To understand why it is so bad to be dominated by feelings, let's take a look at the main situations, with typical examples that almost all traders encounter. We will also see how to deal with these circumstances.

The feeling of fear is usually the first of the emotions manifested by a person who starts trading on the Forex or stock market. Fear can be classified into two types:

- ✓ primary fear
- ✓ secondary fear.

Primary fear

At the start: This fear appears at the beginning, before the first trade. When you study the charts, you look at the quotes and an inexplicable fear begins that the first trade may not be profitable.

Uncertainty: You decide that you are ready for the first trade but immediately a sense of uncertainty arises. What if it doesn't work? What if I'm not ready?

Doubt: Doubt is a psychological phenomenon, a result of critical thinking. In decision making in any life situation, everything is analysed from different perspectives, weighing the pros and cons, and emotions enter the evaluation process.

Chronic fear. In some cases, the fear of the first transaction can become almost chronic: when a person, who has not done anything yet, is afraid to enter the market for weeks (or longer). In the general case, the primary fear is overcome quite quickly, but some people are included in the "risk group", for example the category of traders who are, in fact, afraid of becoming investors.

Here are the main factors that predispose to fear, so that a person who has never traded in the financial markets is able to understand if he is facing a primary fear:

- ✓ Tendency to excessively long and unproductive analysis of situations. It consists of "walking in circles" around the same aspects of the problem.

- ✓ Uncertainty in the decision taken (even when the work is done, we worry).

- ✓ Habit of checking everything several times (if the iron is off, if the child has done all the homework, etc.)

High rigor and a high degree of responsibility towards others.

What to do? How to overcome fear in trading? This can only be done if you understand the reason and mechanism for the appearance of a particular feeling. These are the most common excuses for delaying trading practice due to primary fear and possible solutions in each case:

"I will lose money" - Open the first trade with a small amount. It is not necessary to plan a large-scale or long-term trade to conquer the market. Even if the first transaction is not profitable, assume the loss of this small amount of money as an investment in the business, which will bring good results in the future.

"I don't have enough knowledge. I still have to learn" - If a trader does not have results, positive or negative, it is impossible to truly understand if you have enough knowledge or not. Its quality can only be verified by analysing the results of the operations carried out.

"If I lose the first trade, then it's fate. It's not for me ..." - Fatalism is not the best helper. Operating with destiny in mind is not productive. Don't stop thinking that your first transaction is a litmus test of general success or failure.

"If I lose money, then I am a bad trader" - You will be able to know if you are good or not, after at least 7-10 transactions have been completed. A consistent analysis of the results will help identify any errors and correct them.

"I'm afraid and I can't help it": That's not true, for example,

1. Choose one of the low volatility instruments (for example the EUR / USD exchange rate).

2. Prepare a trading plan. It is desirable that it is short-term.

3. Just click on the corresponding "BUY" or "SELL" button in the trading platform. And don't forget to open reduced positions.

4. As a general rule, in the first few seconds, the heart jumps out of the chest, but almost immediately the pulse returns to normal rhythms ...

5. Don't worry, 99.9% of the time the world stays the same, the computer keeps running, the quotes keep flashing and the market won't backfire on your position within seconds.

Secondary fear

Operations failed. It appears after experiencing failed transactions. Sometimes a small unprofitable position is enough, sometimes fear appears after several failed trades.

Impotence. Secondary fear is stronger than primary fear because it is based on "proven" failure facts: a wrong prediction, a wrong analysis, a wrong interpretation of the fundamental data and, consequently, a loss. Unlike primary fear, secondary fear can make even a very confident person fall into that spirit. If the primary fear is experienced as a feeling of anxiety and doubt about the success of the trade, the secondary fear inspires a feeling of helplessness and demoralization and, above all, overshadows the ability to correctly analyse the market. Therefore, secondary fear affects not only a person's emotional state, but also his intellectual abilities.

Why does fear arise? The emergence of a secondary fear is always due to the negative experience and not to irrational ideas about one's abilities. Therefore, it is more difficult to deal with than the primary fear. This situation is comparable to swimming. If a person has never swam before, they will be afraid of entering the water for the first time. But this fear is more easily overcome than in the case of a person who has nearly drowned in the past. However, each of us realizes that it is much better to know how to swim than not to be able to swim at all. And even if in the second case it will be more difficult to overcome fear, it is still worth doing so, in order not to repeat the mistakes of the past.

The same psychological mechanisms apply to the financial markets. However, here, unlike the swimming example, no one forces a trader to dive into the depths of the market from the very first minutes. It is best to go progressively, in small steps. It's not that scary. However, if mistakes are made and the fear of their possible repetition is established, then it is essential not to succumb to them, everything is repairable.

There is always a risk. Absolutely all traders go through this stage of personal development. Since there are no investors who do not make mistakes, it is impossible to overcome the secondary fear phase, which can only be overcome with varying degrees of effectiveness. Therefore, the "risk group" includes anyone who decides to participate in the financial market.

What to do? To neutralize doubts, it is necessary to understand their essence. Therefore, it is necessary to find out why mistakes were made that led to an unsatisfactory result.

You can determine what has become the cause using the following method:

Take some time to practice analysing the market. A trader should write all his thoughts and predictions in detail in a trading journal for at least two weeks.

From the results of the trading diary, the trader should conclude: how many transactions would have been profitable if they had been completed, and how many would not have been. If according to the forecasts positive results prevail, the mistakes made will be the result of an exclusively emotional impact (for example failure to comply with the trading plan). If the ratio is 50/50, or the number of negative forecasts is greater than the positive, then it is necessary to analyse each trade to understand where the error is.

As a general rule, in these cases, poor performance is due to a lack of specific knowledge. For example, if all negative trades are characterized by steady but small losses, then perhaps the key will be mistakenly set to stop loss orders that the market 'eats' because they are too close to the entry point. Or, perhaps, the trader misinterprets signals from technical or chart indicators. In this case it is necessary to fill the lack of information with the necessary knowledge and find out what are the criteria used and how to set a stop loss or what a shoulder-head-shoulder reversal is.

Trading Psychology: The Emotions of the Trader and typical situations

"I do a market analysis, I make a trading plan, but when I enter the market, I lose control and I don't follow the plan. I get a negative result because I don't stick to the trading plan.

This situation is the most common. As soon as trading starts, emotions are activated automatically and everything that happens on the market is not objectively evaluated.

First of all, technical signals begin to appear and unnecessary information is given a lot of importance. Secondly, the trader believes that it is possible to "control" the operation by intervening on its course (unplanned changes in the trading plan). To avoid this, spend more time working out your trading plan, writing down in advance everything you plan to do when you are in the market and what you cannot do under any circumstances.

"I close the open trades early because it is unbearable to observe a loss. I prefer a small stop loss to waiting for the price to reach the previously set level".

This option is another of the most common forms of fear. A trader has a tendency to close losing trades as soon as the price goes negative.

When deciding where to set a stop-loss order, use not two or three criteria, but at least four or five. Then the stop loss will be more reliable and correct. You will have more confidence that the risks will be proportional.

"I close the trade early as soon as I make a small profit, even though my trading plan is written correctly and tells me otherwise".

In this case, in general, after closing the trade and observing that the market follows the direction, we predicted in the trading plan, we reopen it again. After reopening the position, it closes early. Let's say that, of the 150 points of profit initially foreseen, the trader reaches 30-50 points. Fear can be fought in the following way: as soon as the transaction starts generating income, instead of closing it with minimal profit, transfer the stop loss to the break-even point.

If profits rise even more and break out of the next resistance level, the stop-loss will move even more. Therefore, without closing the position, you will protect your trading activity from any kind of loss.

Trading Psychology - Greed

Another emotion that commonly affects the trader is greed. Generally, greed and fear in trading psychology are opposite emotions and a trader who feels fear is unlikely to feel greed at the same time. Indeed, in the first case, the trader is afraid to enter the market, while in the second case he has an unrealistic view of the market and, consequently, loses money due to his own ambitions. Perhaps the only relationship between fear and greed is that both of these drives can be controlled by a trading plan.

At the beginning. Greed appears in two cases: the trader has a predisposition from the very beginning or appears later following several successful trades.

"I could earn more". The first thought that gives rise to greed is the idea that "I could earn more". Confidence in himself same increases, you think you can control the market and also wants to use aggressive strategies.

Why does this thought arise? The desire to make more money often arises after several successful transactions and the belief that one could have risked more on them.

High risk. Greed is often a feature of successful business and life, of confident leaders. A trader also exposes himself to high risk if his temperament type is choleric.

What to do? It is clear that one cannot change one's temperament, but one can learn to control it and organize one's work in an appropriate way. Here too the trading plan is essential, as in the case of fear. Greed is perhaps the most damaging feeling, because when it appears it inhibits the need for caution.

In short, if the manifestation of fear threatens potential gains, greed increases potential losses. Here are some typical situations in which this feeling is fully revealed:

Forex Trading Psychology - Typical Situations

"As soon as I start analysing the market, I look at the chart and I understand that a strong movement has started. The thought is born: we must act quickly, otherwise I will lose a great moment. The result flies into the market at full speed and only then I understand that was worth".

This is a very common situation, typical of recruits. Even those with an initial orientation towards stable and quiet trading, as soon as they see the price movement "live", are eager to do something immediately.

This can be compared to everyday situations in life. If you arrive at a bus stop and see that the bus left without you, pulled away from the bus stop and accelerated, are you running after it? It most likely doesn't make sense: trying to catch something that moves faster than you. It is much safer and wiser to wait for the next bus.

With the financial markets the situation is similar, only you are not late at all, so there is no reason to chase a bus. To cope with an unbearable desire, we must control our emotions, analyse and elaborate the trading plan. To do this, carefully look at all the charts. Your task is to choose the most suitable opportunity. And for this it takes some time to study the market situation.

Another way to combat the desire to "do something now" is to listen to your inner common sense.

"I have the patience to analyse the market and come up with a trading plan, but as soon as I open a trade and the price starts going in my direction, I immediately understand that I have invested very little money and that the profits could be many more, so I increase the volume of the operation even if it was not planned ".

In this case, the mistake made is a violation of the risk management rules. The initial idea of "I will open a few more lots" usually does not take into account the fact that, along with this, all risks increase exactly as many times as there are lots added to the market. Added to this are unplanned risks.

For some reason, when there is a sudden desire to add something to an open position, it just seems like there will be more profits, and few think the losses will grow in exactly the same proportion.

"When I am in the market and the price is close to my profit level, I begin to doubt that I have set it correctly. As a result, I move it to earn more, because I feel that the movement is not over yet and that I can take advantage of it to earn more. money".

This case of greed is less common than the previous two. It is usually combined with the second option. Traders who are faced with such a desire to hold their position as long as possible do not know the feeling of fear described above.

A different pattern of behaviour is characteristic here, and it differs from the behaviour of "impatient greed".

The trader falls into this mistake because:

- The market is still moving in his direction
- There is no sign confirming the reversal
- The extra ten points won't change anything

The Dow Jones Principle states that price movements are subject to trends: the trend cannot end suddenly, etc.

To be convinced of the wrongness of this position, it is enough to ask: where to transfer the take profit level? where is the most favorable limit? The most likely answer to this question will be "when I get a signal confirming a market reversal, then I will close".

True reversal signals are unlikely to be seen as the trader is dominated by emotions. A frequent end to such greed is the search for signs that confirm the resumption of movement in the right direction and, consequently, the loss of money.

Trading Psychology - Hope

It may seem that hope is a positive, useful and important feeling in human life. How can it harm a trader? Very simple. When a person decides they want to invest, they do so with an optimistic outlook on the future. In fact, whenever we undertake to study something new and interesting, we approach it with a certain positive attitude, otherwise it would make no sense to start something new.

However, as soon as a person starts trading, hope can turn against, shifting from healthy optimism to utopian expectations and belief in miracles. One way or another, it is important to understand what the trader's level of hope is at any given time. A person who does not believe in himself and in his success simply has no interest in being on the market, but he cannot even think that success depends on a miracle or fate. So, what is hope and why is its excess so dangerous?

When born? Hope always arises at the same time, exactly when the transaction starts generating losses.

How do we feel? This feeling is experienced in various ways: a trader who prays to all the gods, mentally talks to the market and does other strange things. The most important negative quality of hope is that it completely captures a person and blocks all possibilities of finally trying to save the situation with the help of mental activity.

The reasons. An open position in the market (or multiple positions) that causes losses. The paradox is that the greater the extent of the loss, the more the feeling of hope shines through and the greater the trader's tendency to believe in a miracle and not in his own strength and intellect.

High risk. One way or another, everyone experiences hope, but for some it is out of control, just like their trading. It is important to be able to control this emotion.

What to do? In general, a hopeful situation can spiral out of control if you don't adhere to a trading plan categorically or if you don't have one at all. If the trading plan is followed to the letter, the trader will not be faced with such a state of hope that he can only count on a miracle. However, if the trading plan is not followed and the circumstances are not favourable to the position, then hope will be inevitable. If that happens, we need to be prepared and take control of the situation and take action.

Trading and Psychology - Typical situations of hope

"I had a trading plan but I was greedy and I didn't close the trade with profits, so I sit and wait for the price to come back, but everything goes against my position ... But I wait and wait ... "

If the trader is not strong enough to correct the mistake and close the trade with less profit and continues to wait for the market to reach its new target, then the situation will reach a tipping point i.e. it may end up going in the opposite direction.

At the same time, the further the market moves away from gains, the greater the hope. In this state, it is typical for the trader not only to believe desperately that this will happen, but also to look for supporting factors. Below are some examples of classic arguments for keeping an open position in the market in the hope that it changes:

- ❖ The Dow Principle says that price movements repeat themselves, which means that sooner or later the market must return to its previous values.

- ❖ The signals of technical analysis say that the market will definitely go in my direction.

- ❖ Success only comes to those who know how to wait

Later, if the transaction remains "negative", the most typical arguments may appear:

- ❖ It can't be that everything is so bad

- ❖ I will not close the trade until the market returns to its previous values

- ❖ Sooner or later I'll have to be lucky.

All these arguments are completely useless and dangerous, as half of them resort to ephemeral things like luck and fate, which have nothing to do with the normal job of a trader. And the other half is based on a subjective analysis, on the search for a confirmation of one's thesis.

"I've been losing money for a long time, but right now the market is starting to change, so I'm opening another position to regain and hedge the existing one. So, I'll win again."

The situation described has a proper name among traders: "tactic to add loss". This tactic is the fastest way to become an unsuccessful trader. The biggest mistake a person can make is trying to recover in this way.

Imagine watching a football match and one of the two teams is losing badly: who would you bet your money on? It is really unlikely that you will decide to bet on the losing team. This same reasoning also applies to the above tactic. In addition to all the other arguments described in the previous paragraph about hope, there is also a part of fatalism about the desire to win back.

It is difficult to fight against this sentiment, because for a trader to close a trade at a loss is to admit his failure. Oddly, most traders are much angrier about this than the loss of money. However, in any case, it is worth remembering that only fools persist in their mistakes, and only fools make no mistakes.

"I have been losing money for some time, but now the situation seems to be improving. I want to wait for the market to reach zero, the break-even level, and then close the position. As soon as the market gives me the opportunity to back to square one, I will close the trade immediately.

The hope that the market will get to the point where it all started is utopian, if only because there is no such point. The equilibrium point is a subjective concept that has nothing to do with the real market.

The error, based on the fact that, being the market a dynamic system, sooner or later it must return to its original position, is obviously false because the concept of 'zero point', 'status quo', in this case, is the value where the loss position becomes neutral. But for the entire market, the "zero point" is a zero price, and nothing else.

Trading Psychology - Euphoria

Euphoria, excessive joy, often arises suddenly, resulting in many positive experiences. The main disadvantage of euphoria is that of falling into uncontrolled joy and, consequently, causing a negative impact on the quality of the analysis.

In any emotional state, the trader's efficiency decreases: as emotions grow, the quality of his mental abilities decreases. Not to mention the loss of the sense of risk and, consequently, the decrease in control over operations. In this case, euphoria, unlike, for example, fear or hope, can be felt by any trader, not only by a beginner, but also by a fairly experienced trader.

When born? Euphoria usually occurs after a series of successful operations.

How does it feel? High mood, joy, pride, the feeling that everything is working and will continue to work. With every successful transaction, trust builds.

The reasons. Every euphoria begins with the joy of a successful transaction. In this case, it is best to assume right away that joy should be expressed as a feeling of satisfaction with one's work, in a moderate way.

The benefit is your salary. This dynamic should be treated this way. Otherwise, for everyone, even a slight fit of joy will gradually turn into euphoria. And several of the following transactions will bring success to the fact that the trader will fall into a state of uncontrolled joy and confidence in itself same. Control the joy and it won't turn into an illness called euphoria.

High risk. Any trader who has completed more than five successful trades in a row or who has increased his deposit size several times in an extremely short time is automatically in danger of falling into euphoria. The only solution is to use special psychological methods to cushion it.

What to do? First of all, learn to approach work with minimal emotion. Second, learn to determine when joy appears and to control it.

Trading Psychology - Typical Euphoria Situations

"Whenever I make a profit, I feel great joy. Sometimes it's out of proportion to the profits made."

Positive emotions are important in strengthening the trader's confidence. It would be strange and wrong if a positive feedback did not generate positive emotions (dissatisfaction with a positive result is a clear sign of greed). Caution should be exercised when:

- ❖ A feeling of joy appears after a more or less positive result, even without following the trading plan

- ❖ The feeling of joy lasts more than half an hour

- ❖ Joy manifests itself in a very violent and excited way.

You can approach this in the following way. To enjoy the success of an operation, it takes some time, about 20 minutes after it is closed. After this time, never open new operations. It is recommended that at least several hours (if it is an intraday position) or at least several days (if it is a medium- or long-term position) pass between a successful trade and the next opening position.

A break from work is a good technique for inhibiting the chemical and hormonal processes that work when a person thinks with his heart or mind. After waiting for a certain amount of time, do not rush to explore new market opportunities immediately. First of all, analyse your success. What was the result of the profit? Did you plan it or was it a coincidence? Did the result meet your expectations? Did you expect more from the market? Did it go as you expected or did you deviate from the plan?

The essence of the analysis, in the end, has to be summed up in one question: are you glad your trading plan worked or had only blown it? If luck has smiled at you, then, in general, there is nothing to be happy about.

"I make money because I always know when to enter the market and when it is time to close the position. I believe this is my method. In the end, intuition is also important"!

This example is much more dangerous than the previous one because intuition is unlikely to lead to real success, which in principle can appear only after six months of stable work on the market.

If the investor is lucky, he can be happy, of course, but in a situation where nothing depends on the trader, you cannot say that we control the market.

"Often, I enter the market immediately after a successful transaction, because I want to strike while the iron is hot. I have had a wave of success and I cannot let it go. Destiny always favours me when I act decisively.

This topic is similar to the previous one. The difference is that this case is even more problematic because it refers to ephemeral situations such as success or destiny. Furthermore, the danger is that seizing the moment means losing focus on risk management and planning. In fact, in this state of euphoria, the feeling of fear is minimal, the risks are not calculated. On the other hand, if we fail, we are likely to attribute it to bad luck.

As with all the cases we have talked about in this article, the most sensible thing is always to have a good trading plan and stick to it. We may not make a profit in the first few days, but it will probably help us not lose too much money and be successful in the long run.

Trading and Psychology - Intuition

The concept of intuition is sometimes overrated and sometimes completely ignored. Let's try to clarify this term, find out what it is and find the best way to use it in trading.

The trader's intuition is nothing more than a subconscious 'file' with all the market information previously made and reproduced by heart at some point. To understand how intuition manifests itself, let's look at how memory mechanisms work. We do this with the following example.

Example of Psychology Trading - Intuition

Suppose a trader has been trading on the currency market for a long period of time with the EURUSD pair (at least six months). One day, just starting to analyse the market situation, after opening the chart, the trader clearly foresees that the price will change. For example, think that the chart will be flat at first and then fall sharply. After that, there will be strong market volatility, where the euro will rise against the dollar, but will not reach the previous highs, and only then will a short but very strong decline in the market begin.

The whole picture of future market movements emerges before him, with so much evidence that one can only wonder where such a detailed picture of market movements comes from. At the same time, the confidence that this will happen exactly like this is 100% absolute.

The relationship between intuition and memory

The explanation of this perception and the ability to "see the future" has nothing to do with mysticism. It is scientifically proven that a person does not forget anything he has heard or seen at least once. Human memory stores absolutely all the information that is obtained in the process of life. The same goes for the information the trader receives from his trading.

All information and knowledge that is irrelevant at the moment is stored in the subconscious, but when a similar situation occurs it can return in the form of a preview of events. For this to happen, sometimes a clue is enough, a similar or identical moment. Therefore, the key point is experience.

The principle of technical analysis according to Dow that "history repeats itself" is based on this phenomenon of human memory and on the phenomenon of the psychology of the multitude (the mental mechanisms of memory are the same in all people).

To develop intuition, a good technique is, at least once a week, to open a clean chart, with no trend lines, no supports or resistances, no indicators, and assess the situation as a whole, visually. There is no need to look for a pattern. Intuition usually appears after 5-10 seconds of study, or does not appear at all. However, we must have operated for at least six months before doing this exercise.

If you analyse the graph for more than 10-15 seconds, the subconscious stops dominating and the conscious mind takes over. We close the chart and move on to the normal workspace, to the standard analysis schemes. Repeating this exercise with different tools once a week can be very helpful.

But overestimating the importance of intuition is not the best way to approach trading. If a trader already has a system to work with, only technical signals, i.e. only objective data, should be a priority in making the decision to enter or exit the market. Intuition as a method can only be used as a 'filter'.

Trading Psychology – Conclusions

To summarize all of the above, let's highlight the main points:

- ❖ Do not enter the market when you are in one of the emotional states we have mentioned.
- ❖ Emotions progress when a trader constantly looks at the charts. Avoid it. After you open a position and have established take profit and stop loss, you go to do other things.
- ❖ It is very useful to leave the monitor once in a while or turn off the computer completely.
- ❖ Do not panic, do not rush into action.
- ❖ Remember that the trader's main enemy is his emotions.
- ❖ Always follow a trading plan.

❖ Do not participate in trading when you are sick or in a bad personal situation: this also implies a decrease in the quality of your work.

❖ Do not listen to the advice of others when you are in the market.

❖ If you have had a leak, don't worry, it's normal. There are no fool proof traders.

❖ The safest way to hone your skills and learn to control your emotions is to trade on a demo account until you feel completely confident that you are ready to switch to a real account.

DIFFERENCES BETWEEN LONG AND SHORT-DAY TRADING

Is it possible to earn with the purchase and sale of stocks and with Forex? We will explain the meaning of going short and going long.

When it comes to investments on the stock market, it is possible to take advantage of short positions and long positions, two techniques that focus on the rise or fall of a stock and which allow you to take advantage of these positions to your advantage.

So, what does it mean to go short or on the contrary go long?

The short and long position in the financial market is an easily applicable "technique" in both Forex and trading. They can literally be defined and summarized as follows.

> Going short: is equivalent to selling a package of stocks;

> Going long: is equivalent to buying a package of stocks;

With the expressions "to go short" or "to go long", we therefore mean a particular mechanism of action aimed, in both cases, to obtain a profitable gain.

They are two concepts related the both the purchase and sale of equity securities, both the action of the currency exchange transaction.

Equities: definition

Equity securities are financial instruments that identify the use of capital as financing of equity or debt shares of a private entity, for example a company. If the entity is public, it is referred to as bonds. In both cases, the securities are profitable in the form of dividends in the first case and interest in the second.

Go short and go long in trading

Often those who approach a strategy linked to an investment in shares for the first time believe that a real gain is possible only if the share actually points upwards. This statement is neither true nor false, as there are many variables that can affect the stock market.

This means that in some cases it is possible to make a profit even simply by aiming down strategically. This is why long positions and short positions come into play, strategies that in the first case are aimed at aiming upwards, in the second downwards.

Going long therefore means buying stocks considering the possibility that their price may rise in the future. This is in order to make a profit by obviously reselling them at the very moment in which their value will be higher than the original purchase price.

Going short or short trading on the other hand means speculating on the fall of a stock through the mechanism of short selling.

This strategy consists in the sale of a package of shares that the investor does not objectively own but which he borrows from his bank, paying them on the basis of their current price.

Short or long: the timing

However, this imposes the obligation to return these shares within a set period (three to six months). It is a period in which, if the share price falls, the investor is required to purchase the same amount loaned by the bank. In this case, paying a lower price and thus making a profit characterized by the difference between the sale price and the repurchase price. Should the price not fall but rise, the investor is in any case "obliged" to buy the package of shares sold again, in order to return it to the bank within the established terms. In this case it does not make a profit but a loss given by the same difference between the sale and repurchase price.

Go short and go long in Forex

In Forex, stocks are replaced by currencies taking into account the relative exchange rate. In this case, going short and going long always assumes a strategic character, however, moved by different dynamics than trading.

Going short - taking short positions: selling a currency pair because the first currency is expected to fall against the second of the pair.

Go long - take long positions: buy a currency pair because the first currency is expected to rise against the second of the pair.

Forex trading: how it works

Let's look at the Euro / Dollar currency pair: if the trader believes that the Euro is destined to appreciate or the dollar to depreciate, he will choose to go long and then buy. Conversely, if he believes that the dollar is appreciating or the euro is depreciating, he will opt to go short or short sell and then sell in order to make the necessary profit. Both strategies can therefore prove to be successful or completely unsuccessful if certain factors and conditioning variables related to the stock or currency market and trading or Forex are not always taken into account: for this reason it is advisable to carefully study the data related to the trend of stocks and currencies of interest before choosing how much, what and how to bet.

Difference between trading and investing

We can say that while trading generally means short-term trading (speculation), investing means medium or long-term investment.

If you want to invest, you can adopt different strategies depending on whether you want to get results in a short time or in a few months or years. If you aim to get results in a single day, you could consider day trading, which consists of open and closed operations during the same trading day. The CFDs allow you to get results on the same day or within a few days or a few weeks.

If, on the other hand, you prefer to invest your money to get results after a few months or even a few years, a traditional investment would be more advisable and therefore in this case you should consider investing more than trading.

The differences between trading and investing

- ❖ Trading is intended in the short term, investing in the medium and long term

- ❖ Trading generally allows you to trade up and down, while investing is only up

- ❖ Trading is generally understood as trading with CFDs, leveraged instruments

So, aren't trading and investing the same thing?

In fact, trading is a short or very short-term investment, so it too is a form of investing. However, sometimes it is preferred to differentiate it from investing as trading is generally understood with CFDs, which are optimal tools for the short term (I'll explain why in a moment).

In general, apart from CFDs, we tend to call trading what concerns speculation, that is, negotiation in a short time that has the aim of "reselling at a higher price", even if it is a bit more complicated than that.

In fact, with CFDs you can trade both up and down, so the goal could be of two types:

- ✓ Close an upward position at a higher price than the opening one

- ✓ Close a short position at a lower price than the opening one

- ✓ With traditional investing, on the other hand, the aim is generally to raise the price of what one invests in. For example, you buy shares with the intent of obtaining a capital gain from their rise.

The financial leverage

CFD trading differs from investing and other asset trading as CFDs are leveraged instruments.

CFD leverage is a mechanism that allows you to trade on a certain value using a smaller capital. For example, a leverage of 1:30 allows you to invest over $ 1,000 in value with just $ 33 of capital.

This is a peculiarity of CFDs, which can be traded through online trading platforms and which have now been very popular in Italy for about ten years. We always recommend evaluating the platforms of regulated brokers, as they are the only ones who can guarantee the correct performance of the service and who obey the Community rules regarding safety, transparency and which offer guarantees on deposited funds.

LIVE TRADING IS POSSIBLE? 10 TIPS TO DO IT

We have all heard the story of a friend's cousin who had a normal life and who started trading and managed to earn millions of euros in a short time.

These stories inspire us and move our hearts.

But in trading it generally depends on knowing what to learn to improve, train and practice trading on a daily basis, working hard to improve your results.

Stories like that of the famous cousin are extremely unusual and sadly unlikely.

There is also another kind of popular story. The story of that great uncle of a friend who made millions in a few days of trading and then lost everything because he was convinced, he had found the holy grail, the key to a living trading, when in reality, he had just enjoyed it for a second. of the beginner's luck.

Unfortunately, we can't wait for the stars to line up in our favour. It is important to understand that we cannot count on completely random events such as luck or expect to be able to live trading from the first day of trading.

Efforts, consultation and determination to make a living from trading

The answer to the original question - can you live off trading - can be obtained by thinking about what you would do with your company if you had one. If you've just started a business, you wouldn't invest in the first project you happen to hear, would you? It would be necessary to investigate and consider various options, since as George Buchananan put it "a fool and his money soon part ways".

Once you're running your business, you wouldn't get carried away. For your business to function properly, you need to plan, set goals, review progress, and take stock.

The same principles should apply to trading. In addition to achieving the goals you have set for yourself, continuing education is essential, and the trading life requires effort, focus and determination.

As Donald Kendall said, "the only place where success comes before work is in the dictionary" (success and work in the original quote).

When you google something like "making a living on intraday trading" you find the stories of some people who made millions in hours. The story of someone who made $ 10 million a year on Wall Street may be true. But what history probably doesn't say is that this person manages billions of dollars in assets.

That $ 10 million is probably less than one percent of the total account he manages. If we compare it to a $ 1,000 account in our hands, the return would be only $ 10 per year!

The vast majority of stories don't tell the whole truth - deliberately at times - so that ordinary people get the wrong impression. Believing that living on trading is easy; but unfortunately, it is not.

Before starting any kind of trading activity, we strongly recommend that you try a risk-free DEMO account. This will allow you to test different strategies, trading techniques, timing, etc. without putting your capital at risk.

The millionaire results we talked about above are very rare. If you doubt the low frequency of successful large-scale trading on Wall Street, also ask yourself how many times a stock trader has been seen publicly reporting their results.

Of course, there are exceptions, but 90% of "big fish " don't publish their results because they are simply not getting great results.

Let's go back to reality: living on trading

There are many traders who believe that you can make money with good capital management and applying the right strategy... only a few actually do. While it is possible to make a living from trading, a lot of training and practice is required.

Many may suffer considerable initial losses because they have enough capital to maintain potential future profit before discovering how to trade efficiently for a living on forex. Therefore, it is necessary to consider minimum capital to live on trading because it is not possible to live on trading without capital to invest and much less without a great and constant education and training.

REMEMBER: You will not achieve your return on investment goals without making the effort to learn how to invest in the stock market. This way you will benefit from the different types of top-notch analytical trading tools that professional traders use. We recommend that you try the tools and train as much as possible to become an efficient trader, before venturing into the world of trading and discovering that only those with solid experience can truly live trading.

10 Tips for Trading A Living

In summary, below you will detail the possible tricks that will make your stock curve bigger and bigger and that will make Forex trading profitable, hoping they will one day take you to live trading.

1- *Living in trading: Leave expectations aside*

The problem starts when some people become obsessed with profit - this anxiety can be one of the main causes that lead to considerable losses.

So, the first rule is to forget about earning goals and above all unrealistic expectations. The idea of living off Forex with a few quick trades is extremely unlikely. Trading that is risky and carried out with too much "presumption" can be one of the causes that lead to losing the initial investment.

This often happens to novice traders who follow the very short-term price action by exposing themselves in a very risky way, so in many cases the overexposure of this group is so high that you lose your capital within a few months.

Generally, the most experienced traders focus on one goal: "To earn the money needed to forget about making more money".

By setting a higher money goal, it exerts a strong emotional pressure on himself same, which could result in one of the largest possible errors that fall into overtrading. We will come back to this concept later.

2- *A living from trading: Define your risk profile*

Gain a good understanding of the fundamentals of the market. If you are not comfortable with dynamics, do not invest in Forex even if it is profitable. This is true for any market.

3- *A living from trading: Choose a trading strategy*

To trade Forex profits, you need to have a defined strategy. There is no right or wrong way to trade, what really matters is that you clearly determine the strategy you will adopt.

To make your Forex trading profitable, try to focus on learning a trading strategy that aligns with your risk profile. Research all trading tools at your fingertips. Study the techniques that seem to have logic and think about how they are used in your strategy. Furthermore, it is possible to study the behaviour of the markets and learn how the industry works.

Finally, if you aspire to a day of trading, don't forget to back test until you trust your strategy.

4- *Living in trading: Don't let yourself be guided by emotions*

It may seem very easy to control them, but it's true: emotions are the worst enemy of a trader who wants to invest in Forex at a profit.

Forex trading is an interesting activity that has a mix of analysis and discipline. You shouldn't blame the market or worry about losing some of your trades.

In order to make a living from Forex, or at least to make your investment profitable, you need to understand how Forex works, trust your own analysis and follow the rules you have established. This is the ultimate key to making profits on the Forex market. Emotions can ruin a trader's experience, so it is vital to put them aside and not involve them in trading.

If you are sad, avoid trading. If you are feeling very happy or excited, avoid trading. Excessive confidence in your operations or a pessimistic attitude can cause large losses.

5- *Live trading: set a Stop Loss and a Take Profit*

Whatever your trading strategy for a living, you should always set a Stop Loss. This type of order allows you to define the closing price of your trade.

Your order will automatically close at this level, even when you are not present. In other words, setting a Stop Loss will give you the peace of mind that you won't lose more than you are willing to risk for a single trade.

However, there may be times when the market behaves erratically and there are price differences. In this case, the stop loss will not be executed at the predetermined level, but will be triggered on the first occasion that the price reaches this level. This phenomenon is called slippage or slippage.

The Take Profit order is an order that limits the initial position and is placed in the opposite direction. For a buy of a lot of 15000 in the EUR / USD pair for 1.2246, the take profit order is a sell of a lot of 15000 at a price above the market price, also taking into account the broker's spread.

6- *Live trading: stay up to date on market trends*

How can you be profitable and start living on Forex? At this point it is vital to keep abreast of press releases and all industry news.

7- *Live trading: Avoid overtrading*

We are convinced that we are constantly finding profitable opportunities in order to achieve our profit goal. Many times, traders may or may not realize this and this is where the self-deception of our mind is at stake.

There are two types of overtrading:

- ✓ That generated by too frequent trading activity
- ✓ The one that involves inconsiderate use of volume in operations

Both types are known to be in many cases the exact opposite of how to make profits and grow with a view to being able to live on trading.

Frequent trading

First of all, let's talk about the problem of operating too often.

In this Warren Buffett talk titled "How to stay out of debt, " Buffett said that discipline is needed when investing:

"When investing, you have to wait to see the opportunity clearly, because markets are not a game."

You can sit back and wait, and if you don't like prices you shouldn't trade them day after day. You could wait one day and then another day, and that's okay.

You can also just wait until you like the prices: this happens when you really know what you are doing. This way, you can really get into the game.

If we follow this same principle in the Forex and CFD market, it makes even more sense.

The conclusion is clear, a trader does not have to do a lot of trading to be profitable in Forex, just do the necessary trading.

When you have a real account, you need to have a strategy with specific pre-set conditions for entering trades. Follow your strategy and don't trade when you want.

High volume trading

The other aspect we have mentioned about overtrading is trading with excessive volume. For many people, leverage is the culprit, but is it really their fault?

As we all know, Forex and CFD brokers offer significant leverage on their trading accounts.

In theory, it was originally to give traders the opportunity to make money on Forex CFDs with small investments. This allows more people to find the value of trading in this market and to use the services offered by these brokers.

However, in practice, using high leverage is still very common among more inexperienced traders who are tempted to maximize their profitability on the Forex market. Although, in reality, what they are doing is maximizing their potential loss.

High leverage does not inherently mean falling into error, as it allows you to trade with larger trading volumes, resulting in the trader having freer margin with which to manage a possible market shift against you.

The important thing is to learn how to avoid overtrading and understand leverage.

8- *Live trading: accept losses*

How to be a Forex and CFD trader and make money consistently? In reality, the word consistent does not mean that you always win over all trades, but rather that in a series of high-level trades you get a positive balance. Closing every single trade for profit is simply a myth.

If we talk about how to consistently be profitable and live off trading in Forex and CFDs for the long term, some professional traders can be consistently profitable on a daily basis, but no one will even be able to show a trading statement that does not include at least one single trade. at a loss.

If you are a losing trader, do not despair and above all do not give up.

The trick is that winning trades are profitable enough to produce enough profits to cover the losses incurred. Keep in mind that this is very common in traders who trade for the long term.

You have to be patient and follow the trend.

9- *Living trading: Create a trading diary*

There has been a lot of talk about discipline in trading, but very little about organization. Following an order leads to consistency and it is consistency that this book is about. It all starts with your trading routine. You need to have a rigorous trading journal that covers most of your trading activity, which will help you reduce the random factor to an absolute minimum.

Many novice traders develop negative trading habits. Like the overtrade we talked about above, where if you start out with any luck, you will continue to overtrade and end up burning your account.

On many occasions, some traders get trades with positive results due to chance or luck, thus reinforcing the possible different negative habits in trading, resulting in the almost impossible to part with these bad habits. How can he be a consistent trader if on several occasions he leaves the result of his operations to chance?

Many traders believe that this luck will not abandon them, but, as everyone knows, luck is not infinite and at some point, it ends, generating consequent losses.

10- *A living from trading: Choose a broker similar to your risk profile*

The best broker is not the one that makes you the most money in Forex. The best broker will be the one with the correct answer to the following questions:

Is it regulated by a relevant financial entity?

Will my money be safe?

What will customer service be like once an account is opened?

Will it be a good forex broker for beginners?

Does it offer a good platform?

Conclusions

Answering this question of how to make a living from trading is very easy. To trade Forex and make profits, you need to buy cheap and sell expensive, or vice versa. It depends on whether your trade is long or short.

Of course, if living on forex were that easy, there would be millions of traders online and no one would ask whether or not it is profitable to invest in the financial markets.

However, the situation is very different. Most Forex traders actually lose money and it is very difficult to start making money on the currency market.

There is no golden rule. Many people look for a straight answer to the question "can you live off trading", and almost everyone ends up using a certain market signal provider. This is an easy way to start being profitable in the Forex market, but we doubt that this profitability will be maintained over the long term.

The main thing to remember is that, in order to be profitable in the Forex market, it is necessary that the value of the winning trades is greater than the value of the losers, even if the losers are more in percentage.

This usually depends on your trading strategy and the risks you are willing to take. Trading on the Forex market is done on margin, which means that the size of your trade can be much larger than the amount of your deposits.

In other words, you can trade for a lot more than you have. This can lead to a lot of money on Forex, although sadly, the same goes for losses.

To make a living out of trading someday you need to have a high level of discipline and a strategy that helps you stay focused and avoid engaging your feelings - the bane of many traders.

The evolution of your strategy will come with use and experience. For beginners it is recommended to trade for some time on a demo account to practice and understand how the market works. When you have gained experience, established a good risk management policy, and created a strategy that works for you, you will be one step closer to being able to make a living from trading.

WHAT ARE OPTIONS

What are Binary Options: example, advantages and risks

We are sure that you too are an online trading enthusiast and as such you are curious to understand what binary options are that everyone is talking about.

If you have any doubts and want to have the best answers, then all you need to do is read what we have to tell you below.

This will give you a clear and simple understanding of what binary options are.

Binary options, or as others call them binary operations or even binary options, are financial derivative products, used by investors, commonly called traders, to speculate thanks to trading on the financial markets.

The activity of speculation aims to profit on the rise or fall of prices, regardless of the value of an asset (stock, bond, currency, index, commodity).

This activity has been hugely successful in recent years, especially since markets have opened their doors to the general public.

Until recently, only insiders could invest and earn in the financial markets.

Today this is no longer the case!

Everyone can access information regarding the performance of any asset being traded, using real-time data that allow you to operate directly on the markets.

Is it worth investing in binary options?

In this period of speculation and economic crisis, the market itself is the master.

The market, in fact, does not count the crisis.

The trader, therefore, taking advantage of the high volatility can profit both if the price moves upwards, and if the price takes the downward path.

By trading with binary options, a single investment can yield more than 80% of the invested capital.

Before listing the merits of binary options let's try to understand what they are and how to use them best.

We have already said that binary options are derivative financial instruments, that is, their value derives from another financed instrument which is called: underlying asset.

The underlying instrument can be a stock, a currency, an index or a commodity.

The binary options have an expiration date and predicting the trader must occur within a certain time limit, obviously chosen from the same trader.

For example, if a certain asset, such as Apple shares, is expected to increase in value, first you establish a maturity, that is, a date by which the price can actually rise from its current value.

If the trader expects that in 4 hours the price of Apple's shares will rise, then he will buy a binary option of the "call" type (binary option to buy) with underlying Apple shares and with a maturity of 4 hours.

Main Deadlines Binary Options

Today the trader can choose the expiry he prefers thanks to the binary options builder.

However, you can also choose between the classic deadlines which are:

- Binary options 60 seconds;

- Binary Options 5 minutes;

- Binary Options 15 minutes;

- Binary Options 30 minutes;

- Binary Options 1 hour;

- 24-hour binary options.

Then there are particular types of binary options called one touch binary options, which can be purchased over the weekend and which offer gains exceeding 500% of the invested capital.

One touch binary option has a weekly expiration, but their trend is more difficult to predict than classic binary options.

Underlying instrument

The underlying instrument can be a stock, a currency, an index or a commodity.

The purchased option exactly replicates the value of the underlying instrument, which means that if you buy a binary call option on the euro dollar with a 5-minute expiry and the euro / dollar exchange rate rises, you earn.

An important premise to make is that investing in binary options generates profits even if the value of the underlying instrument rises by only one cent.

So, it doesn't matter how much it rises, the thing that really matters is that the value of the underlying rises within the set deadline.

Before proceeding further, we wanted to specify a detail.

Easy binary options as many want you to believe don't exist!

They are as serious as the risk of losing or even the possibility of really earning a lot.

Be careful, because you can't always win! After all, it is almost impossible!

Moreover, if the brokers did not have their income, they would not invest millions of euros to open online trading platforms

The risks of losing the deposited capital exist, however, it must also be considered that to earn with binary options you must have one thing in mind: they are not a bet! There are no tricks or do it binary options!

BINARY OPTIONS: PURCHASE AND SALE

Purchase binary options, properly called Call binary options, allow you to earn when the value of the chosen underlying instrument rises no later than the established expiration date.

No matter how much the value goes up, what matters is that this value actually, at the time of expiry, is higher than that at the time of purchase.

Put binary options, properly called Put binary options, allow you to earn if the value of the underlying decreases.

If at the expiry date of the binary put option the value of the underlying has decreased, you will earn in proportion to the invested capital.

How much do you earn with binary options?

The gains obtained with binary options are very high compared to those from any other financial investment activity.

Not all binary options expect the same gains; these in fact depend on the asset chosen, the expiry of the binary option and also the time in which it is purchased.

Obviously, the earnings are clearly visible to all investors, and fluctuate between 75% and 85% of the invested capital.

This means that you can immediately have a very high economic return in a very short time.

Earnings made with binary options can be reinvested or withdrawn according to your needs.

However, we can state that, if you have reduced capital, it is more convenient to reinvest again in order to increase the investment capital and consequently your earnings.

HOW MUCH CAN YOU INVEST IN BINARY OPTIONS

There are investment caps, but they are really very high, reaching around $ 10,000.

Obviously, the maximum amount refers to the maximum capital that can be invested in a single transaction and not the total capital that can be deposited in your trading account, which can also be unlimited.

In addition to the maximum capital, there is also a minimum capital, that is, a minimum amount of money necessary to be able to buy a binary option.

Usually, the minimum sum, said minimum trade properly, ranging from 5 $ to 25 $, and essentially depends on the binary options broker chosen to operate.

MINIMUM DEPOSIT BINARY OPTIONS

In addition to the minimum trade, a very important requirement, there is also the minimum deposit, that is, the minimum amount of capital that can be paid into your trading account.

Usually the minimum deposit is no less than $ 200, but there are still binary options brokers who offer minimum deposits of $ 50 or $ 100.

ATTENTION: particular attention must be paid to the relationship between the minimum deposit and the minimum trade, in fact, one should stick to a ratio that puts only 5% of the deposit capital at risk with each binary option purchase.

Let's take an example:

If the broker offers a minimum deposit of $ 100 and a minimum trade of $ 20, then 20% of the trading capital would be invested in each binary option, which is obviously not advisable, as it would put a much too large part of the capital.

The maximum recommended risk, according to the most modern money management theories, is equivalent to 5% of the total investment capital.

Example of Investment in Binary Options

How to invest with binary options

After this general "coaching" on binary options, let's see in practice how to invest in binary options.

Trading with binary options is extremely simple, with one click you enter the market and you can immediately start earning, let's see together the steps to take to start trading.

1st step: Choice of the type of binary option.

60 seconds binary options: allow you to earn a percentage of capital ranging from 70% to 75% of what you have invested in just 60 seconds.

Classic Options: These are traditional binary options with a variable expiry.

The most used deadlines are:

- ✓ Expiry 5 minutes.
- ✓ Expiry in 10 minutes.
- ✓ Expiry in 15 minutes.
- ✓ Expiry in 30 minutes.
- ✓ Hourly deadline.

One touch binary option: they are very special binary options that can be used on the weekend and have a 7-day expiry.

The gains deriving from one touch binary options are very high and reach 550% of the invested capital.

Obviously, the prediction to be made requires much more experience than a novice might have.

Binary options builder: they are special binary options that allow you to customize your investment to the maximum.

Thanks to this type of binary options you can choose many parameters including risk / return.

The return risk is a very interesting parameter because it allows you to have a refund on losses against a decrease in the percentage of gain.

2nd step: asset selection.

Once you have chosen the type of binary option on which to invest, you move on to choosing the asset, that is, the underlying instrument on which you actually want to operate.

Binary options brokers offer assets that belong to the following markets:

- ✓ Currency market (forex).
- ✓ Stock market.
- ✓ Raw materials market.

With the choice of the asset you can also choose the expiration of the binary option if you have not chosen the type of binary options 60 seconds or binary options one touch.

3rd step: forecast.

This is by far the most important step because it will be the one that will determine the success of the investment.

The forecast to be made is a binary forecast, that is, you have to choose whether the price, no later than the expiry date, can rise or fall with respect to the initial value.

If the price of the underlying instrument is expected to rise, click on the "call" button; vice versa, if the value of the underlying instrument is expected to fall, click on the "put" button.

TIP nº1: we recommend that you always follow the trend of the underlying price.

For example, if the price rises and highlights a bullish trend, that is, a succession of increasing highs and lows, then it is worthwhile to follow this trend by purchasing a binary call option.

If, on the other hand, the trend of the underlying begins to draw decreasing highs and increasing lows, then it is more convenient to proceed with the purchase of a binary option of the Put type.

Once you have made the forecast you simply have to set the amount of capital to be dedicated to the investment, automatically the platform, based on the percentage of profit offered by the binary option you have purchased, calculates the profit you get if your forecast is correct.

TIP nº2: remember to put at risk a percentage that does not go beyond 5% of the capital, per single trade.

The secret of investing in binary options lies in the odds in favour of a given investment strategy to be successful.

Tip # 1 is one of the best strategies for investing and earning in binary options.

Trading with binary options can lead to losses, but in the final balance they will not be relevant due to the greater number of successful investments.

Exposing yourself with an excessive percentage of capital in a single investment assumes a decidedly excessive risk that in the long run will bring more disadvantages than advantages.

If you invest a maximum percentage of 5% on each binary option, the losses will not be significant and will constitute a negligible number compared to that of the profits.

HOW TO INVEST IN BINARY OPTIONS

To invest in binary options, you must register and open an account with an investment platform, commonly called a binary options broker.

The broker offers the possibility to make the investment, providing multiple financial instruments in real time.

The binary options broker, therefore, is the entity that provides the trading platform, the tool that actually allows you to trade online.

Earn money with options

How to register on the broker: binary options trading platform

The first step is to connect to the broker and from the home enter the form:

E-mail

Password

Registration step 1

Registration

The second step is to choose whether to activate a demo account or a real account.

Example of trading with binary options

Asset selection

Here you have to select among the various assets and currencies the one that best suits your strategies.

Choice of time

At this point, you have to choose the time in which the operation will be closed; you can choose between the different options.

Selection of the amount

Now choose the amount you want to invest; the amount must be between $ 1 and $ 100.

Profit in case of correct forecast

If your forecast is correct, at the expiration of the option, you will get a percentage of the amount to be credited to the balance in the event of a favourable forecast.

Forecasting

Now, you need to make your prediction:

"Up" itself we expect that gold prices will rise;

" Down " if we expect the price of gold to go down.

Analyse the price

You need to focus on the current price of the chosen asset.

Transaction closing times

At this point, you need to focus on the closing time and time of the transaction, as this indicates how soon the transaction will close.

Outcome of the transaction

At this point, at the end of the established time you just have to analyse the outcome of the transaction.

If the forecasts turn out to be a success or the operations close in the money, then the asset price has closed at a higher price than the starting price.

Note that binary trading is a system suitable for everyone, albeit very dangerous.

It does not require experts but we always recommend to practice with low investments.

For example, you can choose to invest with the free demo account or the real account of only $ 10 !

BUYING AND SELLING OPTIONS: STRATEGIES AND ANALYSIS

Many investors today are wondering when is the ideal time to sell and buy shares on the stock exchange.

First of all, it is necessary to know well the company in which money is invested, to be informed about the general situation of the stock markets and to also be aware of past trends through the use of stock market charts. Also, knowing how to buy and sell stocks is critically important.

In this chapter we focus in particular on the most effective and easiest to use tool: CFDs (contracts for difference).

Strategies for buying and selling stocks

Study, preparation and training are some fundamental aspects to operate on the stock market and on which to rely to obtain interesting results.

Technical analysis

The first step for a correct approach to buy and sell shares on the stock exchange is to resort to the use of technical analysis, thanks to which to be able to study the trend of prices in the financial markets with reference to past times and with the aim of forecasting future trends, making use of appropriate graphs and indicators.

Technical analysis is today perhaps the most used tool by analysts, together with fundamental analysis, to have useful information and understand when is the best time to invest in the market.

Among the strategies most used by investors, the simplest is to observe the graph and check the performance of a stock. When it reaches historical highs, it is likely to decline in value, as those who bought at the lows will usually sell to secure the profits made. In practice, here is one of the many ideal moments to buy a given type of stock. So be good at following the progress of the stock and seize the right moment to buy the action before it starts growing again.

Stop loss

This is just a trivial example of choosing the correct timing to enter the market. An essential aspect to consider is also to evaluate in advance the maximum amount that you are willing to lose and, in this case, insert a stop loss.

The operation is very simple, as if the stock were to fall beyond our stop loss, the stock would immediately be put on the market and sold, thus significantly limiting the loss. It is widely believed that you should never buy stocks without placing a stop loss order.

To be successful on the stock market, it is essential to establish in advance both how much to lose but also how much to achieve, or the expected level of profit. Obviously, it may be wrong (except in the case of scalping) to sell the shares after the stock rises a few points, but surely you cannot decide to wait for the stock to reach an unlikely price before cashing in the profit, since it was taken as a goal a stratospheric gain.

Of course, if the stock shows clear signs of a rise, it is advisable to let it run and not be impatient to sell. Conversely, if it shows fluctuations for relatively long periods, the sale could be the correct choice to make.

There are many strategies for buying and selling shares on the stock market, and thanks to the use of technical and fundamental analysis it will be possible to understand the best times to buy and sell shares. Of course, to make money on the stock market, the rule to follow is always the same, which is the most famous: limit losses and let profits run.

How the shares are sold

Before even selling a stock, you must first have full mastery of some key factors.

So, let's see how the shares are sold.

Control your emotions

There are good and bad reasons for selling stocks. For example, the stock is going badly, irresponsible leadership and management decisions can lead to the stock collapsing, and therefore making investors decide to get rid of the stock.

Perhaps you have decided that your money would be better invested elsewhere, or you are making losses to offset the gains for which you will have to pay income taxes.

Before selling a stock, review your reasoning to make sure you don't give in to an emotional response that you may later regret.

Do you risk investing emotionally? It might be a good idea to use trading robots.

Decide on an order type

On the sale, your main focus is on limiting losses and maximizing returns.

So, let's see now how to invest from the point of view of timing. The largest investors claim that you should invest for at least 5 years if you are serious about your investment.

As a general rule, you should invest for at least five years. This allows you to have enough time to overcome any market crashes that could cause you to lose your money. If you know that you need to access your money while investing, investing may not be the way to go.

Holding stock in just one company is high risk

Think about it. If this company gets into trouble, you may lose some or all of your money. Rather, you spread the risk by buying shares in numerous companies. This process is called DIVERSIFICATION and allows you to substantially decrease your exposure within a single market, thus decreasing the fluctuations within your online trading account.

It is undoubtedly very exciting to try to place bets on the market, but it is almost impossible that all of your predictions will turn out to be correct, as even the most experienced investors are wrong. Emotional or "unreasonable" trading almost always leads to loss.

Drip Feeding

Instead, you should invest on a regular basis - in investment parlance this is called " drip-feeding " - to offset any ups and downs.

This will give you an added advantage, and the experts know what I'm talking about.

This is how " Drip Feeding " works

If you invested a lump sum of $ 10,000 and bought shares worth $ 10 each, you would have 1,000 shares.

If you bought $ 5,000 for the same stock per month for two months (for a total of $ 10,000 total), you should buy 500 shares in the first month.

EToro 's trading platform is by far one of the largest in the world, as it has grown tremendously after starting to offer copy trading and social trading features.

This is without doubt the best platform currently available.

EToro: What It Is and How It Works

The social features of eToro are what have made this online trading broker more unique than rare year after year within the forex trading and CFD space.

Uncovered Sale

One of the advantages of trading platforms with CFDs (Contracts for Difference) is the ability to short sell stocks (which by no means selling a buy position, then closing it).

How to Sell Shares

Short selling can be induced by speculation or a willingness to protect the downside risk of a long position in the same or a related stock.

With CFDs it is therefore possible to sell short, or therefore to obtain gains even from the decline of a financial market, but also to sell a stock that had been purchased previously.

Same day buy and sell stocks

One of the smartest ways to invest in stocks is to buy and sell within the day. In practice, these are intraday trades that can generate high profits in hours or even minutes.

CFDs offered by eToro or ForexTB are particularly suitable for this type of operation. With CFDs, on the contrary, it is possible to profit on any price difference, so you can earn whether the price of the share has increased or decreased.

The advantage of using the best CFD platforms also lies in the fact that there are no commissions to pay, so trading on the Stock Exchange is even more convenient. On the other hand, if you buy and sell shares on the same day with a platform that applies commissions, you risk ruining yourself!

While it is impossible to invest without risk, CFDs provide exceptional tools to control risk.

Conclusions

Buying and selling stocks is a high-yield investment: contrary to popular belief, even beginners can benefit from it, with spectacular results.

To do this, it is imperative that you use an easy-to-use, safe and reliable investment platform. In this article, we have reviewed some of the best platforms to invest in stocks from scratch.

We also talked in depth about some fundamental tools such as stop loss or CFDs.

Can beginners buy and sell stocks?

Definitely yes. Thanks to CFDs and the best investment platforms, even beginners can buy and sell stocks with excellent results.

How much does it cost to buy and sell shares?

If you use the best platforms like eToro , absolutely nothing because they are free and without commissions.

Unfortunately, there are platforms that apply high fees: we recommend avoiding them.

What are the best stocks to buy?

Those who trade on the stock exchange with CFDs always earn, both when the share price rises and when it falls. So, the best stock to buy is the one that moves the most (positive or negative it doesn't matter).

What is the best bank to buy stocks?

Banks are not an ideal choice for buying and selling stocks. Unfortunately, they always charge heavy fees. Much better to trade with independent investment platforms that have no commissions.

BEST ONLINE TRADING STRATEGIES

The term "online trading" is now widespread and as you surely know it indicates a specific investment method.

Online trading has allowed everyone to invest in any type of financial market, and thanks to the best online trading strategies it is finally possible to enter the markets in an easier way.

Digitization has allowed individuals to directly access various exchanges and exchanges of stocks, commodities, funds, currency pairs and cryptocurrencies.

Obviously, in order to do all this, a Prerequisite is required, registration with an online trading broker.

Among the best known are: eToro , Markets and XTB.

Regulated and reliable, they offer every trader a lot of security but above all a very simple platform to use.

Using these brokers, you will have the opportunity to create and apply strategies that to deepen the potential of online trading.

NB: In particular, if you are a beginner, you should first of all start moving safely on the demo account that these brokers offer.

This will serve to directly ask the brokers initial questions but also explanations on the most useful tools in trading regarding already tested strategies.

Also, on the topic of risk and money management, one of the most important factors for your financial security.

If you are a beginner you could also opt for Social Trading, a new way of trading that will allow you to copy the most experienced Traders!

Before moving on to trading strategies, we want to offer you a general overview of online trading, starting with what it is, how trading works and what risks you could run.

Guide to Trading Stocks

Many investors who are financial experts or simply curious are fascinated by stock trading, this is because identifying a stock that can produce profits is not easy but the challenge is truly engaging and fascinating ...

If your greatest fear is losing your money I should d i make a free test with the demo, does not serve any deposit!

When you decide to start with online trading, usually at the beginning you opt for Day Trading, it is a daily investment.

Practically when we talk about trading, we refer to the trading of a wide range of financial products defined as financial assets such as: stocks, commodities, currency pairs, cryptocurrencies and various derivatives.

The primary goal when you start trading is to take advantage of the price fluctuations of the respective assets in order to generate profits.

Depending on your personal preference, you can choose products with higher and lower leverage, depending on how much you are willing to risk.

By choosing a high leverage, the gain is certainly greater, as is your percentage of loss.

Are there any differences between trading and investing?

Let's say yes.

Trading is designed for the short and medium term, while investments aim to be more durable, such as when deciding to buy stocks.

Let's say that there is no real time limit that separates lasting investments from trading, because there are also those who trade on long terms and manage to reap many benefits.

There are those who are more inclined to invest in dividend stocks that offer regular long-term cash flows, but there are also those who opt for day trading and earn money every day without any waiting time.

Let's say that it is crucial to opt for a trading that allows you to apply individual strategies.

The range of trading tools that brokers offer, such as those we mentioned in the preamble, really include many variations, so that the most diverse requests can be met based on your trading style.

What are your expectations for trading?

There are those who trade it because they are convinced that they can make money quickly and without too much effort.

Let's say it is not as simple as you think, there are in fact many users finding themselves in difficulty abandoning trading.

But there are also those who make trading their real job.

Surely learning to trade is necessary to enter the right dynamics and using a free demo offered by brokers is even more so.

Basically, it is essential to learn how to exploit the most important trading tools because successful trading requires a lot of skills.

There are also those who opt for social trading for which instead of learning to trade independently, they decide to follow the most experienced traders and copy their operations.

This is currently only possible with a trading broker, eToro.

EToro's social Trading (which we have already talked about)

eToro is an innovative and revolutionary broker that thanks to social trading has allowed even the less experienced to access online trading.

Basically, if you are not an experienced trader eToro offers you the opportunity to copy the operations of the most experienced traders.

Let's say that eToro has created a new way of trading online, social trading which is based on the idea that the knowledge of many people is better than the knowledge of a single person, this means that a real network of traders is created. who exchange advice every day?

With the CopyTrader system, beginners are more facilitated, which is why in the last period eToro has registered thousands of subscribers.

EToro's customers are constantly updated on the latest market news thanks to the precious economic calendar that it makes available to all users.

Among other things, it offers virtual $ 100,000 to start trading with Copytrading, it will help to understand how Online Trading works.

What are trading strategies and how do they differ from each other?

If you write online trading strategies on Google you will find a series of strategies that summarize all the practical tactics tried by different traders in different markets.

Certainly, personal strengths, expectations associated with trading and the level of risk vary from trader to trader, also based on the level of experience they have.

The two most used strategies in online trading:

Daytrading Strategy: As the name suggests, this is a trading strategy in which positions are opened and closed intraday (within one day, so 24 hours). This way of trading is certainly one of the fastest but it takes the time to correctly observe the markets in the short term.

By opting for day trading it is possible to use different tactics and methods, in fact it is possible to both follow a trend and decide to trade against it.

Scalping Strategy: The Scalping is a type of short-term trading that has a short duration, usually it's seconds in which you can earn higher figures. Let's say when you scal p ing you decide to opt for the analysis of volatile markets and this requires large volumes reached sometimes only with huge financial levers.

Maximum concentration is usually required because these are open positions that last a few seconds.

To open the trade, you need to look for the right moment. It is a fundamental fact mastery of indicators, oscillators and other fundamentals of technical analysis of the graph.

Why are risk and budget management important in trading?

You should never underestimate risk management because every time you trade you risk money.

Keep in mind that the protection of your capital is of fundamental importance.

It is important to act well and with your head, because when you invest in trading you have to use your own money, so it is essential to consciously take certain risks.

First, the first step is to clarify how much money you want to use as a trading budget and this is the basis for starting.

If you use too much of it, you increase the risk of quickly reducing your broker balance while if you invest too little considering the fees and commissions, exactly the same thing will happen.

So, we advise you to invest around the initial $ 250 to have your back covered.

When you start trading you can also use all the instruments possible to reduce the risk, so the "stop loss " is a good solution.

Why is loss management important in trading?

With trading you can certainly make a good profit, but at the same time you could also lose all your budget.

We want to remind you that losses cannot be avoided in trading, regardless of your strategy you will sooner or later lose money.

It is not mathematically possible to always profit.

However, it will be important to record more profits than losses.

If a success rate of around 40% is expected when you initiate a trade, this means that six out of ten trades will not be correct, this is pure statistics.

But it doesn't mean there will be a loss either.

The most important thing is to have your own trading system to further develop your skills.

Brokers offer free eBooks, training and a lot of information that could be of fundamental importance in your operations.

However, following other traders remains one of the best strategies you can apply.

In practice, we can summarize everything like this:

- ✓ Learn to manage losses because they are part of Trading;
- ✓ Develop a personal strategy based on your needs;
- ✓ If you are not experienced enough, follow the advice of other traders.

What are our conclusions?

We can see trading as a real challenge between you trader and the financial markets.

Regardless of how risk-conscious you are, sooner or later you will surely incur a loss but if you trade with your head and do not get too caught up in emotions you can certainly have a positive balance over the long term.

Learning strategies and especially your training is the first step to improve yourself.

It is certainly very useful to use the offers of brokers and start trading with the help of demo accounts.

Each broker will provide you with virtual capital with which you can try out different types of trading.

Obviously, all this will allow you to understand where your strengths are to be applied in trading.

The trading strategies applicable to Forex

Trading in Forex requires knowing the specific functioning of this market but also knowing the most suitable trading strategies for this type of operation. There are, in fact, various different methods according to your needs and your abilities but also according to market conditions.

76.4% of retail Investor accounts that lose money when trading CFDs with this provider. Consider whether you can afford to take this high risk of losing your money.

Day trading

Day Trading is an investment method that is highly appreciated by Forex traders because it does not require real preparation or special knowledge.

Its principle is to carry out a large number of small trades in a single day and to close all positions before the end of the session. It is therefore the accumulation of a large amount of small gains that makes this investment profitable.

To succeed in your Day Trading strategy, you will need to use significant leverage.

It is therefore essential to know how to cut your losses at the right time so that the total of your gains exceeds that of your losses.

The level of risk is therefore quite significant and you will have to show prudence and above all reactivity.

In principle you have to withdraw your profits within 2% or 3% of maximum profit and above all cut your losses before they reach 10%.

The Carry trades

The Carry Trade method, on the other hand, is reserved for a more experienced audience, being a little more complex.

It consists in using the difference in the interest rates of the currencies between them to carry out a profitable operation without taking into account market developments.

Basically, it consists of buying a currency with a low interest rate to resell it against a currency that has a higher interest rate.

Before embarking on this trading strategy, you must therefore track down the currencies that have strong and low interest rates and you will also have to take into account the amount of the spread practiced by your broker so that it does not take over your earnings.

The Carry Trade also requires a significant investment.

Swing trading

The Swing Trading strategy is another ideal investment method for novice traders because it requires no specific knowledge or thorough analysis. Its principle is very simple and consists in speculating exclusively on trends.

To this end, it is first of all necessary to know how to grasp the strongest and safest trends on the market.

You must then take a position in the direction of this trend as quickly as possible and close your positions when they begin to weaken.

To carry out a Swing Trading it is useful to follow the supports and resistances on the value of the assets.

Forex Scalping

The Forex Scalping strategy resembles Day Trading from all points of view with the difference that in this case it is not mandatory to close all your positions at the end of the day.

But the general principle remains the same, since it consists of making short-term trades in the direction of the trend and making extremely small but large amounts of gains. Again, the amount of your investment must be sufficient to secure your earnings and you must use significant leverage and therefore act prudently by cutting your earnings at the right time.

The analysis of supports and resistances

Recall that a support represents a threshold below which a price fails to fall and a resistance the threshold above which it fails to rise.

The phenomena of support and resistance are therefore excellent indicators that give concrete and reliable information on the different movements of currencies.

To make the best use of these indicators, you will be prepared to use the support and resistance lines. Your goal here is simply to take a buy position above the observed support and liquidate this same position below the observed resistance. However, you can also sell when the value passes below a resistance and buy when it rises above a support.

When starting out in trading it is strongly recommended to draw these support and resistance lines even if experience will teach you to capture them without the need to draw them. The most suitable charts are 4-hour charts and daily charts. These two types of charts are in fact the ones that will give you the best representation of the market trend on the cross you wish to study.

How to draw support and resistance lines

With the help of your graph, you begin to identify the maximum and minimum points.

Warning! To be meaningful these points must appear at least twice on your graph.

Then join the highest and lowest ones with horizontal lines. Each line passes through at least two high points or two low points. You have just drawn the supports and resistances.

Looking at your graph, you will find that some lines pass through more points than others. The more numerous they are, the more these support or resistance lines will represent a reliable index.

And this means that these supports and resistances will have a lot of difficulty in being broken.

So, you just have to take your positions for the sale or purchase according to the phenomena of support and resistance observed.

Recall that the resistances are the sell signals and the supports of the buy signals.

Trend analysis

Technical trend analysis aims to determine when it is preferable to enter the market. For this, consider that the Forex market follows one and only direction in the long term.

We will therefore use monthly, weekly and daily charts in this case.

To use informed trend analysis, you need to determine precisely when a turnaround is likely to occur. When using a weekly chart, it is preferable, before opening a position, to refine your analysis with the help of a 4 hour or 30-minute chart because these two charts will help you track the supports and resistances within these trends.

How to use the indications given for trends

When observing an uptrend, it is recommended to choose an entry point as close to a support as possible. Conversely, if the trend is down, you prefer an entry point close to a resistance.

How to predict a turnaround

There is an effective technique to determine when a trend reversal is likely to occur. For this we use a 10-period exponential moving average combined with a 25-period exponential moving average on a daily chart and a 45-period exponential moving average for a 4-hour chart.

You can thus conclude that: if the long exponential average is located below the short exponential average it is synonymous with an uptrend or an uptrend. Conversely, when the long exponential average is above the short exponential average, we are in a downward period. So when the two exponential moving averages reach a precise point, this point expresses a trend reversal.

Warning! It is useless to rely solely on trend analysis to take a position on Forex. In fact, the information you will get will not be conclusive if not associated with other technical analysis tools, in particular support and resistance phenomena.

The double zero strategy

As we have indicated in the first chapter dedicated to psychological phenomena, investors very often have a tendency to place stop and limit orders on round figures.

Thanks to these indications you can easily implement strategies based on the execution of these orders.

In fact, the amount of opportunities that the currency market offers you increases considerably starting from the moment you are aware of the thresholds in which stop orders are mainly placed because the execution of these orders has the main effect of generating important movements on the market.

This technique called double zeroes is used, consciously or not, by many traders. As a matter of fact, the realization of expectations deriving from the placement of these stop orders often tends to be fulfilled. Here we can cite the example of the acceleration observed the first time these psychological thresholds are reached.

Furthermore, in addition to individual investors, other market players also have a tendency to influence movements linked to psychological thresholds. Traders also use round numbers to place their option barriers. This phenomenon is due to the fact that in the volumes traded on Forex, the part of the exchange options is constantly increasing. Options traders will therefore have the same reaction as traditional traders, passing important orders when a value reaches double zero.

Some advice

You open a buy position at double zero when you observe a downward movement being careful to place a stop order at 20 pips below the entry point and a limit order at 50 pips above this entry point. Similarly, a sell order must be placed on a double zero following an upward movement without forgetting to place a stop order at 20 pips above the entry point and a limit order at 50 pips below. this same point.

Also, in this case, the method we have just analysed, to be effective, must be complemented by other technical analysis tools.

The break-out technique

To profit from this analysis it is necessary to apply it over several consecutive days.

This analysis indicates that it is wise to take a buy position when:

- ✓ the maximums and minimums recorded on the first day of the period were not broken in the following days

- ✓ the value eventually manages to break through the maximum

The break-out technique is particularly suited to the day trading style but will first require you to work on identifying break-out points or breaking points. These break-out points are actually the highs and lows of the first day of the period. To recognize them you must first check that the highs and lows of this first day have not been exceeded during the second and third days. Then just connect them with two horizontal lines, one connecting the maximums and one the minimums.

Finally, to profit from your analysis, you just have to open a buy position as soon as the value reaches the high line or to open a sell position as soon as it reaches the low line.

Some advice

When you decide to open a buy position, make sure you place your buy order 10 pips above the break point. Then place a stop order at 20 pips below the entry point and a limit order at 50 pips above this same point. Conversely, when you open a sell position, take it 10 pips below the break point and place a stop order at 20 pips above the entry point and a limit order at 50 pips below this same point.

Remember that the more volatile the market is, the more interesting it will be for you to open a position on a break-point break. However, pay attention to false breaks which are easily identifiable because they correspond to the supports and resistances of the value.

Thomas Jegu and the "U" strategy

Beginning as an amateur trader, Thomas Jegu quickly gained notoriety for his outstanding performance on the Forex market. Thanks to simple methods and strategies, he quickly knew how to adapt to the currency market and its unexpected events. One of his most popular strategies is certainly that of the "U".

The "U" strategy effectively allows us to identify the most interesting entry points of the market. To get there, just visually analyse the different charts regardless of the market configuration. It then remains to apply suitable Money Management.

How to find a U configuration?

To best identify a "U" configuration it is necessary to use 3 different types of Japanese candlestick charts. One to 4 hours, one to 30 minutes and one to 10 minutes.

The first allows us to analyse the underlying trend, the second the short-term trends and the last the medium-term trends.

This analysis shows a possible movement of overbought or oversold than one value, and then to take advantage of the correction phase that follows.

More clearly, "U" configurations always follow the direction of the trend. So, if the underlying trend is up, the "U" configurations will be played on buying and inversely when the trend is down.

To correctly identify these configurations, it is first of all good to identify an upward or downward rally of the various values, that is, one or two successive candlesticks, upward or downward. (Attention, the shadow of these candlesticks must be greater than 100 pips over 4 hours, 80 pips over 30 minutes and 60 pips over 10 minutes). We then have to wait for two or three consolidation candlesticks to form, which will somehow give a signal of the end of the upward or downward trend. Finally, as soon as the trend corrects 25 pips over 4 hours, 20 pips over 30 minutes and 15 pips over 10 minutes, it is synonymous with a buy or sell signal.

Once this identification can therefore open a purchase position using a lever effect that goes from 5 to a maximum of 20. Place then a stop order 20 pips below the lowest point of consolidation candlesticks and a limit order to livell or where the decline was confirmed. Of course, in the case of a longer-term operation, it is good to increase the thresholds for stop and limit orders.

Some advice

To take as little risk as possible, make sure you have at least three consolidation candlesticks before opening a position. Do not trade except in the direction of the trend because the inverse remains too risky and never forget to place your stop orders to avoid too large losses in the event of a market reversal.

LET'S START: TRADING ONLINE

Very often beginners think that online trading is complicated. It's not true. Once you understand the concept that you can earn both when the price goes up and down, the more is done.

In practice, to do online trading you need to predict the future trend (in the short term) of a financial security. There are several ways to do this:

Technical analysis: the price charts of the financial stock are analysed in search of specific patterns that can help make a correct forecast.

Fundamental analysis: the fundamental economic situation connected to the financial security is analysed to make forecasts. For example, if we want to make predictions on the performance of a listed stock, we can analyse how the company is doing. Or if we want to make a forecast on a currency, we can consider the overall economic trend of the country.

Copying the best investors: it is a technique that has always been used, observing what great traders do to reproduce their strategies. Today it is possible to use automatic Copytrading techniques thanks to the eToro platform.

Trading signals: In this case we follow the instructions of a financial analysis centre (which can use very sophisticated techniques of fundamental analysis or technical analysis). These signals can be sent by email, SMS, WhatsApp or Telegram.

Obviously, beginners tend to start mostly by copying the best ones or by operating with trading signals (both solutions are great). Among other things, observing what the great traders do or the forecasts of the large financial analysis centres has a very high educational value: it is probably the best way to learn online trading!

Technical Analysis

What is the technical analysis? Why is it so important for trading? How can you increase your earnings through it? If you are looking for an answer to these questions you are really in the right place.

This is the most complete introductory guide to the topic of technical analysis of financial markets. Let's talk about the most important discipline for studying the prices of goods, securities, cryptocurrencies and any other asset in circulation.

For decades, online trading professionals have used technical analysis to steal the secrets of market trends. The best ones manage to reach incredibly high profit heights and boast an excellent negotiating ability.

Thanks to the power of technical analysis, a character like Warren Buffett (a true legend of the markets) has earned the nickname of the Oracle of Omaha. This nickname was given to him precisely because with the help of technical analysis, Mr. Buffett was able to make market forecasts that no one else could ever have imagined.

This powerful means of investment is now available to all traders thanks to the best online trading platforms.

Technical analysis: reading behind the lines of the markets

Before continuing, better clarify a concept immediately. There is no analytical technique and no trading strategy that can make a trader earn 100% of the time. Trading online is a form of investment like any other and therefore exposes you to the risk that your operations may go wrong.

However, the point is that with the help of good technical analysis the trader is able to chart a course to follow. This route in most cases leads to profit, but only on condition that all the calculations and the necessary preparations have been made well to arrive at the result.

Have you ever wondered why it seems that most of those who trade online lose?

The reason is very simple: they have a tendency to carry out operations without following any criteria, without having any operational plans. The pattern followed by most losing traders is always the same: hitting the buttons on the platform at random in the hope of making a profit.

It goes without saying that no one has ever earned anything by behaving this way. If you don't follow a trading strategy, if you don't do preliminary analyses that anticipate market trading, trading turns into a 100-hourly race along a foggy road.

What traders of this type don't realize is that the fog hides a wall and sooner or later you end up on it and end of the race. To earn with trading, you need a different attitude, you need a strategic, prepared and success-oriented attitude. All this can also and above all be guaranteed by the use of technical analysis to read behind the lines of the markets.

Technical analysis: definition and functions

After this introduction aimed at underlining the importance of using technical analysis, let's talk about this discipline in more detail. First of all, it is necessary to define well what technical analysis is.

The term technical analysis defines the activity of studying the price charts of market assets. By asset we mean any asset, security, commodity, currency or cryptocurrency that can be traded in online trading today.

Whoever works as a technical analyst is therefore responsible for analysing the historical price trend shown by the charts on specialized trading platforms and sites. The study of past data allows the trader to make predictions on the future price trend with excellent accuracy.

It is thanks to the conclusions drawn during the technical analysis that the trader decides which strategy to use to make money by investing in this or that financial asset. In particular, you can decide to:

- ✓ Open a buy position in case the price is growing

- ✓ Open a sell position in case the price is falling

The theoretical basis of technical analysis

Technical analysis can be conceived as a real science and as such it is reliable. Its theoretical foundations, without going into technical details, had been dictated by Charles Dow. For this reason, still today, we talk about Dow's Theory, a man who in his own way and in his time laid the foundations of technical analysis.

Here are the 6 basic foundations of technical analysis as laid down by Charles Dow:

1- The 3 phases of the markets

The 3 main market phases according to Dow are primary, secondary and minor trends. The primary trend is a larger trend that lasts more than a year. The secondary trend is a trend of intermediate duration that can range from a period of three weeks to one of three months.

The secondary trend often moves in the opposite direction to the primary trend. Finally, the minor trend of a market lasts less than 3 weeks and can be associated with the movements of the secondary trend.

2- The phases of the trends

The second principle of the Dow Theory explains that market trends have and follow 3 different phases. The 3 types of trend phases are called accumulation, speculation and distribution.

3- The market discounts all news

The third principle establishes the strength of the news towards the market. Dow was the first to theorize that the market is strongly affected by all the news concerning it and moves in the wake of the impact that the news has had. This means that any market (commodities, Forex, stocks, etc.) discounts all news concerning it as soon as they are released (to know the news, it is good to consult the economic calendar).

4- The market indices are confirmed

Dow argued that stock market indices, or stock baskets, must be correlated as having the same exposure under current economic conditions. For example, the Dow Jones must have a correlation with the Dow Jones Transportation Index. If there is any kind of divergence, Dow argues that there will be a trend change on one of the indices, so it is difficult to predict where this new primary trend will start or if it will develop. If, on the other hand, there is a correlation, then a confirmation of the trend is generated.

5- Trends are confirmed with volumes

When we talk about volumes, we refer to the amount of money invested at a given time in a market. The increase or decrease in volumes is a very important indicator on the markets. If important volumes accompany the formation of an upward or downward trend, this is a strong and positive signal on the continuation of that trend. If we are in the presence of low volumes, however, the trend could still be valid, but it is not representative of an overall vision.

6- The trend continues until reversal

Trend reversals are the worst enemy of any trader in a trade. You have to recognize them immediately to get out of your position promptly and take home the profit.

However, the sixth and final Dow Principle states that a trend remains confirmed until there is irrefutable evidence to the contrary. That is, all the necessary analyses must be done before establishing whether the trend is over or not.

Technical analysis: is it too difficult?

Given what we have hinted at so far regarding technical analysis, a question might arise: is it too difficult a discipline for beginners? Doing technical analysis is far from impossible. Of course, we are not talking about a very simple thing, but even a novice trader can easily do it.

The most important thing for those who want to trade on the financial markets is the practice, especially the practice of technical analysis. Learning to use the basic analysis tools doesn't take too long. It takes about a week to master the main trading tools available on all trading platforms.

In fact, technical analysis is done through the so-called "technical indicators" or that series of models and charts that help the trader make decisions on the market. With technical trading indicators you receive a lot of data and indications on how and where it is really convenient to invest alone.

On the main trading platforms, it is possible to operate even just by observing the simplest indicators and leaving them with the default settings. Later, when more experience has been gained, the trader can also decide to change the basic settings to customize the operations. But this is to be postponed to the moment when you are really ready to manage it in a conscious way.

Our advice is to focus on learning and using only one indicator at a time, starting with the simplest ones such as the " simple moving average ", which is already a powerful tool, although very easy to use.

The two main currents of technical analysis

Among those who use technical analysis as their main source of data to operate on the markets, two main currents can be distinguished: theoretical analysts and practical analysts.

Theoretical technical analysts represent that kind of perfectionist traders. They spend their time analysing down to the smallest and most insignificant market movement in the belief that they can predict and understand whatever is happening on the price. The theoretical analyst is almost never satisfied with the results of his analyses and continues to extend them over time to the point of risking losing important trading opportunities.

Generally speaking, it can be said that the less experience you have in trading, the more you tend to be "theoretical analysts". For us this type of approach to trading is counterproductive because it is dictated by the fear of making mistakes. Perfectionism in trading doesn't pay. Better to spend hours on the demo account making mistakes in the market readings and settings on the platform, rather than living eternally waiting for the presumed right conditions to operate.

The other current is that of practical technical analysts. This is the type of trader who, once objective data has been collected from the indicators, does not hesitate even for a moment and opens his market position. This is an attitude that especially those with good experience on the markets take. In any case, it is the right attitude, the winning one, especially in the long term.

The operational principles of the practical analyst are only 2:

- ✓ Enter the market as soon as a trend is recognized
- ✓ Avoid trading when the market is on the side

In the end, the rules for success in the investment phase, as you can see, are not difficult to follow. Also note that the simpler, clearer and more direct they are, the easier they are to follow.

Becoming a practical analyst: the demo account

Do you want to become a practical analyst too? Well, then know that there is a tool that can do for you and that is offered for free to all new members of the online trading platforms: it is the demo account.

The demo account is a trading account designed only to practice and therefore understand how trading and the financial markets work. As we have seen, practice is essential to become a trading ax and always know how to read the various market situations, so using the demo account is really crucial.

Specially to learn technical analysis, the demo account presents itself as the ideal tool because it places the trader in front of price charts in real time with the possibility of opening and closing positions based on their own analysis at any time. All this can be done without fear of making a mistake, because the demo account contains only virtual money and therefore losing it does not cause any problems, it is only for practice.

Technical analysis: price charts

Now let's go into the detail of that element that is the basis of technical analysis, which represents its soul and fulcrum: the price charts. When trading, the activity takes place almost entirely on specialized trading platforms and able to offer price charts in real time.

If this is the case, it is obvious that every operator must necessarily specialize as much as possible in the ability to read graphs and must know everything about them. Charts are great because they contain virtually all the information a trader needs to be successful in investing on their own.

Almost every single symbol or formation that is created on a price chart has a meaning and offers the trader information that he can exploit to his advantage. Regardless of the market in which you operate, price charts are always important. Whether you like investing in stocks, Forex, cryptocurrencies or commodities makes no difference.

Price charts: how do they work?

Each of us at least once in a while watches the news. Very often in the course of the broadcast we also talk about finance and markets and for this reason the price charts of some financial asset or security are also shown. Charts are still used today because they represent a maximum simplification of the price trend and make it immediately readable.

Of course, for those who have never seen one, the signs on the graphs could also seem like meaningless lines, indeed for someone they could just look like hieroglyphs. But these signs are actually gold for all financial traders. the charts show the past of the price and their trend can also express what will happen in the future.

On a chart, what you look at is nothing more than the graphic representation of the price, but always within a specific time frame.

The 3 types of charts for technical analysis

In any form of online trading there are only 3 main chart types and these are:

- ❖ Candlestick or candlesticks charts
- ❖ Bar charts
- ❖ Line charts

These three types of charts can be interchanged at will on all the best trading platforms. Sometimes changing the type of graph serves to receive information that cannot be obtained on the other type and vice versa, but it is above all professionals who know how and when to change graphs.

In addition to the X and Y axis which represent the basic elements of each graph being the space and time variables, there are two other fundamental elements that characterize a graph:

- the time frame: the "time frame" is the specific time frame at which we want the graph to record price changes. In simpler words, a daily time frame will show the prices of the financial instrument under examination on a daily basis, an hourly time frame will instead show on an hourly basis and so on. There are also monthly and yearly time frames.

- volume: volume is the total number of trades during a given period of time. This is usually a trading day, but depending on the time frame you set to analyse a chart you can observe the trading volume at 1, 5, 15, 30, 60 minutes and so on. The greater the number of trades, the greater the volume. By observing the trend of the volume, we can identify the emergence of a trend just as we already do with the price.

Let's now analyse the 3 main types of graphic representation, namely candle and sticks, bar and linear.

The candlestick chart for technical analysis

The candlestick chart is also often referred to as candlesticks. This is certainly the most widespread type of chart and this is because candles represent a real mine of precious information. Thanks to the data they provide, the candles can be used for any trading strategy starting from the simplest and short-term to long-term ones.

Candlestick charts are distinguished by one main feature: their effectiveness in making market turning points understood. This is a crucial aspect for any trader. Furthermore, they are also used because they give great margins for reducing operational risk, a constant concern especially for professional traders. But we are sure that even beginners don't like to lose money, so it's important to remember to use the candlestick chart.

In the candlestick chart, every single symbol you see on the chart contains valuable information such as:

- the opening prices;
- the maximum and the minimum;
- the closing price.

Many traders confuse the candlestick chart with the bar chart because they notice some similarities between the two types, but in reality, there are not many similarities, as, in the candlestick chart it is easy to notice the presence of a "main body" which instead is absent in the bar graph.

This part known as the "real body" of the candle is used to identify the differences between the opening and closing session of trading on a specific day. Candlestick charts are much simpler and more readable than other types of representation, in particular the following rules apply.

Rules for reading the Japanese candlestick chart

To interpret them you need to follow some basic rules:

- the length of the bar indicates the difference between the opening and closing prices;
- the colour indicates the trend of the stock, or whether it is down or up.

In the charts of the trading platforms of the best online trading brokers, the colours of the candles can be black / white, or red / green.

In any case, distinguishing the candles will be simple because the black and red colours indicate a bear market, while green and white indicate a bull market.

To date, most brokers prefer green or red candles, which are considered much easier to read and graphically more appealing to the eye.

A candlestick chart provides more information than a linear chart, as the latter only signals the change in the closing prices of the security examined, while the former allows you to grasp its performance, trends and even anticipate its future situation.

Bar chart and its elements

The bar chart is also quite easy to understand because it is made up of more or less the same elements as the candlestick chart. The biggest difference is that the bar chart doesn't have a colour that distinguishes the candles.

This type of chart is mainly used by traders who intend to trade on standard time intervals. Precisely for this reason they always try to set the graph to show all possible details within the preferred time horizon.

What is the bar chart made of?

The bar chart is also referred to as open high and low close. Here, however, the market trend that is bullish or bearish is not indicated by different colours. This is because opening and closing are indicated by a horizontal segment that protrudes to the left or right of the bar, respectively.

✓ When the opening is lower than the close then there is a bull market

- ✓ when the opening is higher than the close it means that the market is in a bearish phase.
- ✓ When the opening and closing coincide, the market does not have a precise direction but it is a very rare case.

Looking at the bars, the upper end of these represents the maximum, while the lower end represents the minimum. Even in the case of bars, the difference between the two values is able to determine the volatility of the reference market. The bar and candlestick charts are much more comprehensive and offer much more information than the line chart.

Line graph: the simple representation

Traders do not always prefer complex representations, sometimes it is necessary to access only basic information concerning the market and, in this case, it is sufficient to rely on the cleanliness and clarity of the linear chart.

With this feature of lightness and cleanliness, the linear chart is able to immediately express the presence of an upward or downward trend or to show trading volumes in a given period of time.

This type of chart is used by all those traders who consider the closing levels of the market to be much more important than the opening ones.

However, as most traders prefer intraday strategies, the linear chart is very often ignored in favour of the other two types we have talked about. Often one is forced to resort to it especially if information such as market opening or closing is not available, in this case observing the graph helps to get an idea of the historical price trend.

The problem with these charts is that they aren't always 100 percent reliable.

How and how much do you earn with technical analysis?

As we have seen, technical analysis is that key tool that allows you to be guided in the investment activity in a rather immediate and direct way. However, the burning question that every trader asks himself is how much he earns with the technical analysis of the financial markets.

The answer in this case is: it depends. There are many factors that can affect the results obtained and these vary from trader to trader and also based on the trading strategies you choose to use. In any case, to start you must first look at the trading capital you have and not to suffer losses.

As we have seen in this guide, technical analysis offers a statistical advantage. In other words, with the same quality of analysis carried out on a market, a trader of average skill can make a profit in 6 out of 10 operations. Now, based on the availability of an initial capital of $ 100, we can say the profits in such operations can range from a minimum of 5-10 dollars to a maximum difficult to establish.

On average, a trader with such a small starting capital can think of taking home between $ 30 and $ 40 per trade if he is able to enter the market in the trend phase. Otherwise things get complicated and the gains start coming more slowly.

But beware of potential loss-making transactions. Very often 4 out of 10 trades close at a loss and this can cause damage to your investment capital. For this reason, the rule that all professionals in the sector follow is very simple: never invest more than 5% of the capital in any single market operation. This is a great way to avoid losing all of your investment capital. To be able to prevent this from happening you must remember to exit the market at most after having suffered a loss of 5% of the total capital: this means that you must close the position at a loss of $ 5 if you have a total capital of $ 100.

Trading signals

Before concluding, it is appropriate to talk about trading signals. Many traders use them because they are unable to do technical analysis or fundamental analysis on their own. What are trading signals? They are indications on potentially profitable market situations generated by experts or by financial analysis companies. Of course, not all trading signals are equally reliable. Among other things, there are free and paid trading signal services.

Technical analysis conclusions

In this long guide you have got to know the potential of the greatest discipline practiced today in the field of online trading: it is technical analysis.

Thanks to this activity, even novice traders can think of starting to make money with their trading operations made on the various financial markets, however it is important to practice a lot and always apply the principles of technical analysis without thinking twice.

Finally, remember that technical analysis is nothing if it is not carried out also with the help of a good trading platform, so it is also important to choose your platform wisely.

What is technical analysis applied to trading?

Technical analysis consists in studying the prices in the chart with the aim of making correct predictions about the future trend of the Asset.

Does technical analysis work?

Like all forecasting tools, it is not infallible, however if properly used it can give investors a lot of satisfaction.

What type of Trader uses technical analysis?

All trading professionals use technical analysis as a decision support, regardless of their operation.

Who was the inventor of technical analysis?

Scholars trace the origins of this analysis to Charles Dow, an American analyst who also gave the name to the famous Dow Jones index.

Better technical analysis or fundamental analysis?

They are two complementary methodologies that must be used together to perform at their best.

Fundamental Analysis

What is fundamental analysis? Here we will talk about fundamental analysis and how this discipline can impact the trading activity of any financial operator.

Why did we decide to dedicate an in-depth guide to just the subject of fundamental analysis? Because this type of analysis, together with technical analysis, represents the starting point for achieving any degree of success by trading online.

The truth is, few traders have heard of it and really know what fundamental analysis is. But it is precisely because of ignorance of such determinants as this that most traders lose capital. Wanting to trade without knowing fundamental analysis is like wanting to row without oars: it's practically impossible.

Given the importance of this indispensable topic, we decided to create a content that explains the basics of the subject in a simple but effective way. Doing fundamental analysis is not impossible and it is not something reserved only for professionals in the trading sector.

Anyone can do it and increase their results in the field of online trading and when we talk about results, we mean profits! This certainly seems like a good reason to continue reading the guide. For this we invite you to invest a small part of your precious time on this page. Because the time spent learning something new is always an investment (especially in the trading field where knowledge is power).

Fundamental analysis: what is it and how does it work?

We want to keep the speeches as simple and gradual as possible. We realize that for many readers the concepts of trading, if too many and too technical, can be indigestible. So, let's start from the ground up, here's a definition of fundamental analysis:

Fundamental Analysis refers to the discipline that studies the market trend of assets based on macro events and data, but also on any other external factor that may influence the price trend in the future.

From this definition you can immediately guess some things:

Fundamental analysis is a study; therefore, it is a scientific discipline, which proves to be reliable in most cases where it is applied to online trading.

This kind of analysis basically makes it possible to make forecasts on financial markets. This does not mean having the power of foresight, but it does mean being able to estimate with the greatest possible approximation what could happen on a market based on information from concrete data.

By studying any factor that can influence the performance of a market, this discipline allows the trader to make projections on what could be the next market development and therefore it will be possible to study the most adequate and least risky trading strategy below, based on the price movements that can be expected.

Any professional trader makes use of fundamental analysis, without exception. Perhaps only those who use extreme techniques such as Scalping can afford to ignore fundamental analysis. However, this is only possible because one chooses to operate in the very short term with techniques at the limit. Otherwise fundamental analysis always remains the ideal option.

Fundamental analysis and markets: a close relationship

As we have already detailed, traders have 3 basic time choices to trade the markets:

- ✓ Invest in the short term

- ✓ Invest in the medium term

- ✓ Invest for the long term

If for the short term many traders prefer technical analysis (using indicators such as Elliott Waves and others) for any other investment time horizon the fundamental analysis remains simply… fundamental! There is certainly no shortage of traders who also prefer it for short-term operations, but in principle fundamental analysis gives its best results especially if used to invest on the medium and long term.

For professionals who use it every day, this discipline is an art form. This is because for fundamental analysis to be effective it must be accompanied by the right interpretations. But what does this mean? Doing analysis always has a discretionary component that depends on the interpretation that the trader offers of a certain event or phenomenon.

Giving the correct interpretation of events is the only way in which fundamental analysis can be truly effective. In fact, the cause / effect correlation on the markets is not always immediate. This means that event X will not always lead to consequence Y. For this reason, whoever does fundamental analysis must be good at offering the right interpretation of the facts to make the right decision.

Thankfully, in most cases, the annual cyclical events and news that are known to affect the markets almost always have the same effect. Even where a beginner may find it difficult to understand what the effects of a given news could be on a given market, there is always the possibility of going to check in the past what happened when that same event occurred.

For this reason, those who use fundamental analysis have an optimistic view on online trading.

The role of macroeconomics

It is no coincidence that fundamental analysis is also known as macroeconomic analysis. These terminologies are used because the market studies that are part of fundamental analysis have almost all to do with macroeconomics.

As reported on Wikipedia:

"in economics, macroeconomic theory (or simply macroeconomics) is a branch of political economy which, unlike microeconomics which studies the behaviour of individual economic operators, instead studies the economic system at an aggregate level".

It is therefore a generalist and universal field of study that studies the big to get to the small, that is what happens on the single financial market where the trader is willing to make investments and of which he is required to know the market movers.

In essence, therefore, macroeconomic analyses determine all the global factors that can impact the demand and supply of a given asset.

The price of an asset, in fact, whether it is a share, a currency or a raw material, is always determined by the law of supply and demand.

This is why fundamental analysis is effective on any type of market and financial asset, without any exceptions. It can be used both to understand what will be the future trends of the largest and most important market in the world which is Forex, and to study, at a more specific level, all the factors that influence the prices of a specific company on the stock exchange, for the purpose to understand if his shares will appreciate or depreciate.

Fundamental analysis and market correlations

How is it possible to do macroeconomic analysis and really understand what will happen on a certain market? How is it possible that fundamental analysis allows us to make such precise forecasts on market trends? All this is possible because the market is like a great all-encompassing system. A single, perfectly correlated whole.

Especially today in the globalized world in which we live, markets are completely linked to each other. To give an example, it will suffice to recall how the Greek crisis of 2009 threatened to bring down the entire economic system of the European Union with a great domino effect.

But these mechanisms and effects are equally powerful on a global scale as well. Just think of what happened in 2008 with the sub-prime mortgage crisis. That phenomenon that started in the United States of America was leading to a generalized default on a worldwide level. Only with a great deal of effort have central banks been able to contain the damage.

The correlation of the markets

Correlation is one of the key factors of fundamental analysis. I know deals with the measure of the relationship between two variables. Correlation can be divided into two types:

- ✓ it can be positive and in this case the variables move in the same direction

- ✓ it can be negative and in this case the variables move in the opposite direction.

In short, it is a proportional or inversely proportional relationship. The "correlation rate" indicates how much the two variables are related and influence each other. A classic example of correlation concerns bonds. Let's take the case when bond prices and bond yields are inversely correlated.

When bond prices rise, yields fall and vice versa. In this case we speak of a negative correlation between price and yield. Financial markets are full of correlations. And professional investors pay close attention to them. As long as a certain trend lasts, the correlations (positive or negative) between the performance of stocks, currencies and commodities are a reference point for understanding how to move and therefore how to earn.

Professional traders, those who earn the most, are able to intercept before others when some correlations jump and to grasp the emergence of new correlations, new trends that are born before others. Thanks to this ability, they can dramatically increase profits. But the interesting thing is that learning correlations is not difficult, especially since there are some standards.

Fundamental analysis as a trading tool

As we will see shortly, technical analysis is the counterpart of fundamental analysis and there are traders who lean towards one or the other discipline. Anyone who chooses to set their action on fundamental analysis to be successful in online trading is called a fundamentalist.

This figure has always been framed above all in the stock market, i.e. the market where the shares of large companies such as Facebook, Prysmian or Nike are traded. The fundamentalist's job, therefore, has always been to analyse the growth potential of a company to establish the convenience in buying its shares.

Here are the 3 main approaches to trading fundamental analysis:

MACROECONOMIC CONTEXT ANALYSIS: as we have seen, in this case the assessments are made on a global basis and concern the different main economic areas distributed over the various continents, this way it becomes possible to determine the markets in which to invest.

SECTORAL ANALYSIS: secondly, there is the sectoral analysis which more specifically concerns the business prospects of a given economic sector. The analysis in question requires specific knowledge of that particular sector, or in any case a good ability to access sources is required. In this case, the evaluations can go beyond the economic and financial factors because the sectors analysed can be the most varied (nanotechnologies, biotechnologies, high tech etc.).

COMPANY EVALUATION: finally, with the technical analysis, as we mentioned earlier, specific analyses are made on individual companies, which is an excellent approach even for the small novice investor. Here it is necessary to analyse public budgets and therefore build solid opinions on what the intrinsic value of a company can be. Once this is done, a comparison is made with the evaluation expressed by the market, this can lead to recognizing the overvaluation or undervaluation of a company. This is where investment decisions start.

Invest in equities with fundamental analysis

Here's a little insight into how to invest in the stock market alone with the support of fundamental analysis. We go into a little more technical details on how these analyses are carried out, but the novice investor will not have to worry much about the difficulties in making these evaluations because very often they are made available ready-made by professionals in the sector.

In the first instance, to invest in equities you can use the approach of the company valuation according to the balance sheet indices which are 3:

Solidity index (DEBT / EQUITY): here we are talking about a very important index because it describes the relationship between financial debt and equity. It expresses the firm's dependence on external sources of finance and also the firm's vulnerability to changes in interest rates. In short, this index is able to make people understand the real solidity of a listed company.

Profitability Index (ROI): this is the ratio of operating profit to invested capital. It serves to quantify the ability to generate income with the typical activity of the company.

This index can be considered satisfactory if it exceeds the cost of borrowing. In this case it is convenient for the company to borrow money to invest it in the characteristic activity (leverage).

Global profitability index (ROE): ratio between net profit and shareholders' equity.

It expresses the ability to remunerate equity and is a synthetic indicator of efficiency. It is satisfactory if it exceeds the rate of return of risk-free investments (government bonds).

Economic Indicators for Fundamental Analysis

If originally, therefore, fundamental analysis was considered above all the prerogative of those who operate on the stock market, now the approach has changed because scholars have realized that the AF method can be used in any other market with full success.

Below we go into the question of economic indicators, that is all those parameters that can influence the price of an asset during its market course. Keeping them under control can help you understand the right time to buy or sell currencies, stocks and other financial assets.

In short, economic indicators are nothing more than data and statistics useful for making stock market forecasts on specific time frames. Thanks to them it is possible to extrapolate the growth estimates of a given market for the following months. The information produced by the indicators is exploited by anyone who uses fundamental analysis as their workhorse.

When analysing a market to understand what type of investment is necessary, the best strategy is to compare and put together the results of one or more indicators. If the data of many indicators coincide and all go in the same direction then this is a strong signal that can indicate the future price trend with good accuracy.

On the main economic indicators that we are going to discuss, not only the traders make the decisions, but also the political decision makers and it is precisely in this way that the economy influences politics and vice versa. This is the fascinating world of macroeconomics and determines the present and the future of governments and nations that cannot ignore economic indicators to make their decisions. Traders must do the same (they can also help with the economic calendar).

GDP: the role of Gross Domestic Product

It was 1971 when the economist Simon Kuznet received the Nobel prize for economics. In part, his victory was also due to the invention of a new indicator destined to have a huge impact: GDP or gross domestic product.

GDP plays the key role in quantifying a country's productivity and its ability to produce wealth. It is therefore not a method of measuring wealth itself, but the ability of a nation to produce it. GDP can be thought of as the market value of all final goods and services produced by a nation.

Thanks to these characteristics, the GDP is also considered as an indicator of the well-being of a nation. This is also because GDP is often accompanied by a comparison with the national public debt, as the gross domestic product is an indicator capable of defining the ability to repay the debt itself.

In general, a State can have a high public debt, but also a high GDP (e.g. United States) without thereby incurring situations of financial danger or risk of insolvency: what matters is the relationship and the reciprocal trend of the two quantities, as the GDP in this case represents an index of how much the State is able to restore its public debt through, for example, taxation and related tax revenues.

GDP data is reported 4 times a year and represents the sum of all goods and services produced by a nation over the year.

If the GDP does not grow, it is evident that the nation is not growing either and this has an impact on trading because negative data on GDP very often also carry negative trends in markets such as:

- ✓ Banking market
- ✓ Stock market
- ✓ Forex market

Conversely, if the GDP is growing, the markets are positively affected and a climate of confidence is generated on the financial stability of a country.

Work: employment data

The data on the trend of the labor market are very important for those involved in online trading. Especially for those who trade on Forex it is essential to know them and understand what kind of impact there could be on the markets of interest. Employment data is important because it too reflects the general performance of a country's economy or specific sectors of it.

The interpretation of a given economy is also made by counting the jobs that are created. You also need to know what percentage of the workforce is actually employed and also the number of people who are actively looking for a job. Finally, the numbers of those who applied for unemployment benefit must be added to all these data.

The main indicators on the labour market are:

Unemployment rate: the unemployment rate indices are released once a month and speak of the results of all the surveys carried out by sector scholars who examine the situation of companies and citizens. The rise in unemployment must always be seen as a warning that must be put on the alert, on the contrary, a decrease in unemployment is always good news.

Employment rate: This is the other side of unemployment and indicates the number of people who found employment during the previous month.

Claim for benefit: This figure shows how many people have applied for unemployment benefit in the reporting period.

This indicator therefore talks about how many people have lost their jobs and need the subsidy to support themselves. When the labour market does not work, this data has a great impact on the markets.

The employment data are very important in fundamental analysis because they allow us to understand in which state the national economy is located, but also the spending and consumption capacity of the people, which in turn affects the state accounts.

On the other hand, when the data indicate an increase in jobs, the data can be taken very positively and so can the growth of the price of a currency or of companies that are in the sector from which the positive employment data come from.

The weight of inflation

Inflation also has an incredible weight in the field of Fundamental Analysis. This is an indicator that can become a real obsession for some countries, given the weight it has on their economy. Central banks, on the other hand, make it the fulcrum of their monetary policies, a reference point to follow capable of guiding their work.

What exactly is inflation? This is the change in relative prices expressed in percentage terms. It is detected in a given reference period and at the lowest point of the supply chain: that is the retail trade, this means that to know it it is necessary to refer to the prices of products and services as they reach the consumer.

To calculate it, the prices of consumer goods are taken into consideration. It is therefore a basket elaborated by experts that generates data on the two main types of inflation:

Overall: this kind of inflation is the one that takes into account the set of standard goods.

Core: the other type derives from the word "core", ie the one that considers the products and services that have the most volatile prices.

Inflation greatly impacts the currency market and the whole real economy.

First, it impacts supply and demand. When prices tend to rise, demand increases because the consumer wants to secure the good before the price goes up again, in the same way when prices fall there is a tendency to delay the purchase because one is sure to have the economic availability even in future and therefore the demand is lowered.

In trading, inflation has an impact in the short term, and therefore must be taken into consideration by those who keep their positions open for a short period of time, and even by those who engage in intraday.

From this point of view, inflation is composed exactly like a medium-high power market mover. In the immediate future, it has the power to disrupt market trends.

As any forex course explains, inflation is also a major driver of the currency market.

Balance of payments

We are now talking about balance of payments or the registration of transactions that are carried out by residents of a certain country with respect to the outside world. We are talking about a pure and simple accounting indicator that aims to detect the transactions that are carried out between the residents of an economy and non-residents over a given period of time.

The balance of payments is made up of two accounts:

Current account: refers to the count of goods and services

Capital account: Refers to the purchases and sales of financial and real assets such as stocks, bonds and real estate.

The balance of payments is useful because it helps to determine how the economic flows of a country are going, for example it can help to understand if a certain nation is attractive from the point of view of investments or not taking into account the capital that comes from outside.

The trade balance (BOT) is expressed through a simple equation which is the following:

$$BOT = \text{total exports of country X} - \text{the total imports from country X}$$

Surplus can occur on the balance of payments, or that situation in which there are positive data. This means the country in question is more dependent on exports than imports.

At this moment in the world countries such as Canada, Germany or Japan are able to boast a trade balance with surplus. This is because they have healthy economies and can enjoy higher savings rates.

On the other hand, when the balance of payments is in deficit, the accounts go into deficit. This means that there is a shortage of exports in the given country. However, a negative deficit is not always associated with negative reactions from the markets. Often it can only be due to natural business cycles. It is no coincidence that important countries with enormously expanding economies such as the United States and China have a deficit balance.

The Public Debt Factors

Finally, a mention of public debt as an important factor for fundamental analysis cannot be missing.

When public debt increases this must always be a cause for concern for a government. Especially if we are talking about already heavily indebted countries, the increase in debt can represent a strong sign of economic instability.

This figure represents the total value of the debt accumulated by a state that is financed through the issuance of government bonds. This factor is not to be confused with the "deficit" which instead represents excessive outgoings from the state coffers compared to annual revenues.

The Treaty of the European Union states that every nation should have a debt of no more than 60 percent of its

GDP. But this threshold has already been abundantly exceeded by many European nations.

Fundamental analysis conclusions

The world of finance and markets is split in two. On the one hand there are strong supporters who think that the best and most reliable way to trade is to choose fundamental analysis, many others believe that to be successful in trading one must rely on technical analysis.

As we have seen in the course of this or chapter, fundamental analysis is already in itself a small universe where it is possible to learn and have a lot of useful data to invest. Similarly, technical analysis represents another side of the same coin.

It is impossible to say which approach is better than the other, but perhaps ultimately it is also a rather stupid dispute and an end in itself. The important thing is that everyone uses the tactics and analysis strategies that he prefers and that he believes will lead him to the result as often as possible.

The best approach is that which involves a balance of the two forms of analysis. The two approaches should be combined and also used in parallel in order to obtain the most reliable data possible and then think about investing.

What is certain is that by using the principles of fundamental analysis presented here, for decades there have been traders able to make significant profits and bring home the desired results, thanks to an effective analysis strategy and model.

We conclude by recalling that those in a hurry to start without problems can always use the eToro platform that allows you to automatically copy the best traders in the world. There is also the possibility of subscribing to some good forex signals service, but in this case, it is necessary to verify that the signals generated are really good.

Trading Signals (Reliable)

What are trading signals? They are indications on market situations that can suggest winning trades to traders. There are various types of signals. To give a trivial example, for those who do technical analysis, reaching a maximum or a minimum can be the signal to sell short or buy.

Most novice traders are unable to do technical analysis themselves and therefore need someone to provide them with the right trading signals at the right time.

Trading signals is a great idea, at least in theory. In practice, most of the trading signal services available on the market are not reliable at all and therefore could cause you to lose money. Furthermore, in many cases these signal services are paid and therefore to the detriment of losing money with trading is also added the insult of having to pay!

What does the word reliable mean?

It is very important to make a clarification: reliable signals are not those that guarantee 100% of operations that close in profit. Unfortunately, there is no such service in the world because it is impossible.

Financial markets are unpredictable and no one is able to make 100% correct predictions. Therefore, even the most reliable signals service could give wrong signals. It is not a problem: the important thing is that the number of good signals (which lead to operations that close in profit) is greater than the number of those that lead to operations that close without profit.

Scam trading signals

Be very careful: many scammers offer trading signal services (usually for a fee) promising 100% reliability of transactions. Basically, these characters are selling (at a high price) a method of making easy money.

When looking for trading signals on the internet you must always be careful, very careful. The promise of easy money can lead some naive beginners to fall into the trap of these scammers.

We can define them as fake gurus who promise 100% reliable trading signals, in exchange for a payment.

These are not trading experts (in fact, they have probably never traded in their entire life) but they are great at marketing, in the worst sense. Very often they also falsify their signal service history in order to show high gains in the past (which actually never happened).

Falling into the trap is dangerous: not only because you spend money to buy something that doesn't work but also because those who follow these fake trading signals end up losing money.

Paradoxically, it is good that many of these services never send even a signal to their subscribers: in this way at least, they do not lose money with completely wrong market operations.

It is therefore advisable to carefully analyse the reviews of a trading signals service before starting to use it

Telegram trading signals

In recent times, the fashion of looking for trading signals on Telegram has spread. In this case, only the medium in which the signals are distributed changes, not the substance. Most paid signals hide scams and don't work.

The use of Telegram serves above all to protect the privacy of those who sell them and therefore to secure them from any actions by CONSOB and the judiciary.

Traders, on the contrary, should prefer signal providers who operate transparently, following the regulations that serve above all to protect their money rather than venture into the no man's land represented by Telegram.

YouTube trading signals

YouTube is apparently the opposite of Telegram, as the videos are published online and are therefore publicly available. The videos posted on YouTube, in any case, contain rather vague trading signals and of no practical use.

Usually the owners of these YouTube channels use publicly available videos to capture attention and then propose paid services, with more precise signals.

In practice, in this case YouTube is not the method to distribute signals but it is only a form of marketing. The quality of the distributed signals, in fact, can also be very low in this case.

CFD trading signals

Why is it convenient to trade with CFDs? CFD stands for contracts for difference, these are financial contracts that offer various advantages to traders:

- ✓ They are simple to use

- ✓ They do not require the payment of commissions

- ✓ They can be used with leverage

- ✓ They allow you to start trading with small amounts

All these advantages make CFDs the best tool to invest in the financial markets, especially when you have a small amount of capital available.

Trading signals or automatic trading?

Trading signals should not be confused with automatic trading. In the case of automatic trading, in fact, the trader does not have to do absolutely anything and the operations on the market are carried out directly by the broker through various mechanisms.

There is the possibility of using trading robots, i.e. algorithms developed in a specific programming language, for example MQL4 for Metatrader 4.

Or there is the possibility of using Copytrading systems such as the one developed by the broker eToro which allows you to automatically copy the best traders. In this case all the trader has to do is select the best traders, the Copytrading software will be responsible for replicating, in real time, all the operations made by these traders.

Indeed, eToro's system is one of the few automated trading systems that actually work, even for beginners.

The difference between automatic trading and trading signals is clear: in the case of signals, the trader receives an indication of a market situation.

It is he who has the responsibility to decide whether to follow the indication or not, by placing an order on a broker. In the case of automatic trading, the system automatically carries out the operations, without the need for constant intervention by the trader.

In any case, even when doing automatic trading, the trader is responsible for the operations performed. In the case of eToro , for example, it still has to choose the traders to copy and has to check, day after day, that these traders are making profits.

Trading school

Very often the use of trading signals is seen as a way to make easy money when you have a low level of experience and knowledge. They can actually lead to some profit (if you have the intelligence to choose reliable trading signals) but it's probably not the best way to use the signals.

We must never forget that following a good trading signals service is an excellent trading school: a way to learn online trading by observing concrete situations in detail.

We can say the same thing about eToro's automatic trading: many novice traders use it for educational purposes, to learn online trading by observing live what the best traders in the world are doing.

Technical trading signals

As we said from the beginning it is possible to obtain trading signals also manually and this is made possible thanks to the tools of technical analysis.

Of course, this is not a simple discipline open to everyone. In reality, although anyone can learn to do technical analysis, it is undeniable that this takes some time to be assimilated in the best way and exploited properly.

Some trading experts claim that it takes even 5 years to master this which is considered by many to be a real art. In our opinion this is not exactly the case. Let's explain better.

It is true that technical analysis is a very broad field, but it is also true that it is also true that it is not necessary to learn all the technical analysis to be able to trade successfully by getting valid and effective trading signals on the markets from time to time.

In most cases it is enough to learn a few basic indicators, even just 2 or 3, to be able to obtain results by using them extensively for your market operations.

But how exactly does technical analysis work?

Trading signals with technical analysis

Technical analysis allows you to make forecasts on Forex or other financial markets by studying past price data.

In practice, we go to study the past to have the opportunity to understand the present and predict, at least in part, what will happen in the future on a certain financial market, be it that of a cryptocurrency or that of a Forex currency pair. Of course, do not be under the illusion that in the field of trading it is really possible to "predict the future" all that can be achieved is an excellent approximation of the direction that the price could take. The important thing is that your forecasts are true in most cases, so in the long term your investment portfolio should certainly have a positive trend.

Where are the signals coming from?

Here, as we said, technical analysis is useful as it is capable of generating trading signals in favour of the trader, that is, it is able to indicate the exact moment in which it is convenient to enter the market and with what type of position it is necessary to do it.

Not only that, because technical analysis through its technical indicators can also say much more. For example, it is able to suggest when a certain market is about to run out of trend and shows signs of reversal.

Such data also helps to understand when it is necessary to exit the market, in case a position had been opened on the previous trend in progress. But there are many other data available thanks to technical analysis such as:

- ✓ Market volatility
- ✓ Price convergence and divergence
- ✓ Market contraction and expansion
- ✓ Volumes of participation
- ✓ Price trend

In short, you can get a lot of information that ultimately helps to improve your investment results. Learning technical analysis, therefore, is very very useful, but if you want to start earning immediately it is better to rely on the solutions proposed before.

Example of signals with the moving average

Here, now let's go into more detail to talk about technical trading signals that can derive from the simplest indicator ever, or the moving average.

Briefly explaining the moving average, we can say that it is a curved line that can be displayed directly on your price chart.

Its shape depends on the past of the price of the asset you are analysing and it follows the market trend purifying it of the so-called background "noise", which prevents traders from understanding exactly what is happening.

Let's see a picture of the moving average to understand what it consists of and an example of its many technical trading signals.

In this picture you can see 3 clear bearish signals which have been generated by the price and moving average directly. All clearly legible and easily interpretable.

The image is taken from the chart of the Eur / Usd or the euro dollar, the famous currency pair where it is very convenient to invest due to its volatility.

Here are the trading signals present here are even 3. The moving average is represented here in green, while the price is in the form of red and green candles, or the classic Japanese candles.

Whenever the price exceeds the moving average with its red candle from top to bottom, the bearish signal is generated and in fact, as you can see, the signal occurs.

The price actually falls for a certain period of time, decreeing the strengthening of the euro against the dollar. But when does such an operation allow you to earn?

When a Short operation was opened, or a sale, when one of the 3 signals was generated, then a capital gain would be realized.

Typical situation:

Let's say you are on the euro dollar chart and follow the moving average. The first valid trading signal (and also the best one in the image analysed here) occurs when another red candle forms immediately after the first one that has crossed the moving average.

Here, this is the classic trading signal confirmed by the birth of a new bearish trend that actually never stops. Similar signals can also be obtained with other indicators such as hichimoku.

In fact, on this graph it is also possible to trace a bearish trend line, that is a trend line that clarifies how a downward trend has actually been triggered to be exploited with a "sale" investment with CFDs.

Here is a case study that features 2 trading indicators together that confirm the bearish signal: the price bounces on the bearish trend line 3 times confirming that the trend is very strong, and it could last also because the trend line is not very steep.

This is a clear case where when doing market analysis with very simple technical analysis tools it is possible to obtain reliable trading signals. Experience then does its part by indicating to the trader when it is really appropriate to enter the market.

Learning to use moving averages and trend lines in any case is not very difficult and with a little practice it is possible to make many successful traders using these tools to obtain confirmed and reliable trading signals.

Conclusions

Trading signals can be a great way to make positive trades in the market but you have to be very careful not to fall into the traps of unscrupulous scammers who sell signals that don't work on the internet.

An excellent alternative to the trading signals is represented by Copytrading of eToro: in this case you can select the best traders and automatically copy all their operations.

Both trading signals and Copytrading , in any case, can be used profitably for educational purposes, to improve the knowledge of trading.

Are trading signals effective? It depends on the supplier.

How do trading signals work?

The general operation is to receive a notification in real time about when and how to enter the market. A sort of real-time assistant to operate at best.

Are trading signals free?

It depends on the company offering them. Some are paid (even thousands of euros per month), others are totally free.

Do Trading Signals Really Work?

There will never be certainty of profit, the important thing is to choose suppliers with a high percentage of return.

FAMOUS TRADERS, NAMES, STORIES AND STRATEGIES

The stories of successful traders are always a source of inspiration. Especially for those still at the beginning, these stories are a way of observing how high this activity can be. If you have had a bad day on the markets or are excited to have just entered this world, here you will find the collection of stories that will energize you to face the markets.

Ed Seykota

Ed Seykota is an American trader born in 1946, famous for his achievements and his books. Over the course of 12 years, he has turned $ 5,000 into over $ 12,000,000 trading commodities.

His approach, by himself, has been called " Aha!". This is the typical exclamation you make when you realize you have just understood something, nothing more. According to Seykota, in fact, the best way to predict the trend of raw materials is the simple reasoning. There is no precise path, but a simple light bulb that lights up in the trader's mind and suggests what to do.

When not using reasoning alone, Seykota is based on a very simple strategy: following the trends already in place. It may seem like a trivial advice, being a fundamental of trading, but it is true. Together with some collaborators, Seykota was among the first to build an automatic trading algorithm; the algorithm, based precisely on following the trends already in progress, has made a large part of its fortune.

George Soros

Few investors are as iconic as G. Soros, who has become a legend in the industry. In addition to having generated a financial empire for itself, it has also done so for the clients of its funds.

The philosophy of this trader is unique in the world. Soros makes little entry on the markets, but tens of billions of dollars have come in which completely change the price balance. When it sees a clear window of opportunity to take advantage of a trend, it does.

For example, its operations on the British pound and the Italian lira are historic. George Soros' funds have not only generated billions of dollars, they have literally written pages of financial market history. It is certainly not easy to trade following his philosophy, given the amount of money required, but his remains a history of speculation like no other.

Jim Rogers

Jim Rogers was one of the most forward-looking investors at the turn of 2000 and 2010. His entire career has been particularly praiseworthy, but this decade heralded his best achievements.

The story begins in 2002, after the crisis of. com. For the uninitiated, it is a historical speculative bubble based on the shares of digital companies that were emerging in those years. After the speculative bubble burst, the US government decided to implement various policies to get the economy back on track.

Rogers realized that the exit strategy from the recession was causing two other speculative bubbles: one linked to the personal debt of consumers, the other linked to the real estate market. This is why he decided, in 2006, to short sell large quantities of some securities. The shares sold had in common the belonging to some sectors:

✓ Banks and the mortgage market in general;

✓ Home builders and other real estate businesses;

When the stock exchanges collapsed in November 2007, due to the explosion of these two bubbles, Rogers collected record figures. Then he began to devote more attention to investing in China, one of the many topics on which he published a book.

There are few brokers that allow you to invest on indices and Chinese stocks. If you want to join Rogers to invest in the largest market in the world, however, there are solutions.

Steve Cohen

Steve Cohen's story is one of the most beautiful.

Cohen was first successful as a trader for some big names in the world of funds. Later he founded his own company, which immediately reached important goals. Its success was daily, not tied to a particular event.

Cohen's trading strategy, even today, is quite aggressive. Its traders have a lot of exposure to individual fund positions; the operations are intraday and with a mixture of buying and selling short. For "normal" people, his figure is one of the most approachable sources of inspiration.

But be careful, because not all that glitters is gold. Over the years, S. Cohen has come under the SEC's sights multiple times. This commission has accused him of insider trading on several occasions. In particular, an operation involving two pharmaceutical companies, which earned Cohen $ 250 million, remains an unsolved mystery.

David Tepper

David Tepper is the founder of Appaloosa Management, one of the most respected companies in the world of investment funds. When he makes a statement in public, which is often the case in his CNBC interviews, all eyes of finance are on him.

With $ 12 billion in personal assets and over $ 13 billion in assets managed by his funds, few have any doubts about his prowess. Its trading strategy is based on the intrinsic value of companies. A strategy very similar to that of Warren Buffett, which we will now illustrate better.

Tepper encapsulated his strategy in a phrase he often repeats: "Few people got rich with their seventh best idea, but many people got rich with their best idea. " Based on this principle, your fund invests in very few highly selected stocks.

In 2020, 50% of Appaloosa Management's portfolio consists of just three stocks: Alphabet (Google), Amazon and Facebook.

It sounds absurd, but it really is.

Simon Crackwell

Another trader of the generation born between 1945 and 1950 who has achieved an amazing success.

Crackwell is known for its short selling.

His company invests a lot of resources in studying companies that risk going bankrupt within a few years.

Once the stocks in question are identified, sell positions are opened which almost always end with a huge profit.

This strategy is based on highly calibrated market revenue. During times of crisis, it is one of the best ways to increase the value of your portfolio.

In addition to having won several front pages for his arrogance, he is famous for having a remarkable calm. Even when the markets move quickly, it doesn't break down; waits for the right moment to place the right investment.

Crackwell had a brilliant career, but his highlight was shorting a large American bank. Having identified his weaknesses, he opened a short selling position close to a billion dollars; its success was total, because the bank went into receivership after the attacks of 11 September 2001 on the World Trade Center.

John D. Arnold

JD Arnold's story begins in 1995, as an employee of Enron. At the time, Enron was one of the biggest names in the world in the electricity industry.

His work earned the company $ 750 million, all of which was made by trading oil. He succeeded thanks to speculative trading strategies, based on technological methods that were not very widespread at the time. Arnold used the internet, the algorithms and systems that were pioneering at the time.

After Enron's bankruptcy due to one of the most scandalous false accounting events in history, Arnold founded his own investment company. Until 2012 he managed to make profits between + 178% and + 315% per year, until his strategies became obsolete. Seeing the change in the world of financial markets, Arnold decided to end his company's adventure to retire to private life.

What do the stories of famous traders have in common?

All the traders we have listed use different strategies and different methods to manage their market revenue. But in some respects, their stories are similar.

All of them started from scratch: some as a private trader, some as an employee, but all of them started without big capital. They have dedicated themselves to the financial markets' day by day, regardless of the small initial failures. It is worth noting that, among other things, almost none of them immediately started making money.

What made the difference was certainly the ability, but even more the constancy and determination. Put yourself in front of the charts every day, trying to understand them thoroughly and to anticipate the next price move; this is the spirit that drives every famous trader story, and it is what every trader should do.

Quality of Famous Traders

Consistency, determination and commitment are the most important qualities for a trader!

As you can see, the strategies of these traders are all different. This is what we mean when we say that there is no universal method of investing that is valid for everyone. Each strategy has the potential to make a profit, as long as you are able to hone it and make it better day after day. From Forex to commodities, each asset offers the opportunity to make profitable investments.

If you want to walk in their footsteps, this is the way to go. Open your account and start investing, starting with the demo account and then moving on to the real one. Day after day you will build the skills you need to make your climb in this world. The road may seem long at first, but few sectors can give you the same satisfaction.

Are traders favoured or disadvantaged today?

Many of the famous traders we mentioned in the guide are certainly not youngsters. This may make you think that trading was once easier than it is today.

In reality this is not the case. Famous traders are older because they have stood the test of time. There are stories of traders who have had great success, but which only lasted a few years. If we're talking about people who have made billions (or tens of billions of dollars) over several decades, it's clear that stories like this have a different impact.

In hindsight, it is easier today to be successful in trading than it was yesterday. You can invest directly from home, without having to spend years as an employee in an investment fund and without needing to have your own company to have access to the markets.

Trading used to be expensive with traditional channel fees. On each position, a minimum of 1-2% ended up in the hands of intermediaries. You can now pay a fraction of these costs. That's why today, if you really want it, is the right time to write your trading success story.

Who is the most famous trader in the world?

George Soros, known for earning $ 1 billion in a single day and for having undermined the entire British financial system with a single operation.

How much did famous traders earn?

Depending on who we consider, the figures range from $ 750 million up to $ 14 billion in a career.

What are the strategies of famous traders?

Each famous trader has a different strategy. This shows that there is not a single "magic" strategy that works in online trading.

www.ingramcontent.com/pod-product-compliance
Lightning Source LLC
Chambersburg PA
CBHW071359210526
45465CB00001B/166